Heartless Ambition

A shocking, suspense-filled plot that explores vengeance, abuse and covert racism.

BEVERLY A. MASSEY

Edited By:
Beverly Massey

Printed By:
IngramSpark

Printed in the United States of America

First Printing Edition, 2022

ISBN 979-8-218-05161-7

Table of Contents

Author's Note

Here I am at the age of 90 believing that I can write another book. I really do love to dream up scenarios and try to get them into some kind of enjoyable reading. Hence, my husband, my children, our ten grandchildren, our thirteen great grandchildren and the few friends I have who are still standing, have tolerated my efforts for the last many months.

My first try at fiction writing, a novel titled **TARNISHED**, was a modest success and received positive feedback from the Readers' Favorite organization as well as many readers. This has led me to continue with the general background of a small New England town and its' many examples of people's similarities the world over.

I have attempted to include the foibles that arise in many of us as we try to survive, prosper, and still be human and humane. This has not been as easy as it would appear.

In **HEARTLES AMBITION** there are two main characters; one who works constantly to become successful using his own merit, and one who is constantly manipulating others on his road to success. Both men touch a lot of people along the way; Chance doing his best to overcome an abusive childhood, and Andre trying to rise politically without scruples.

The resulting disastrous "meeting of the twain" brings readers and townspeople the problem of deciding which life style is to be tolerated. It is my sincere hope that my readers will enjoy the narrative and end up investigating their own beliefs.

INTRODUCTION

The car drove quietly through the town, noticed by just a few. After all it was 7AM he told himself. Still, he was sure there were quite a few of Branfield's early birds not missing the moment. He knew that Branfield had become a highly sought after bed-room town and many needed to get on with an early commute. That would mean that HERMS would be full. He immediately alerted his crew not to use Main Street but to approach the station from the seldom used Oak, instead.

He thought he might be saved scrutiny, though, because the citizens were accustomed to seeing his police car cruising the city during the early hours. The department had made a thing of it months ago in an effort to keep the citizens pleased with their security and their police department. There was no way he could imagine what a field day the press was going to make of this hot day in June 2022, he knew.

"I swear." The police chief muttered aloud. "What would the gossipers think if they knew exactly what he was doing? No one would believe this; I can't seem to absorb it myself."

There were two black men sitting quietly one on either side of the back seat of his car. He had been told that they were very famous but had to admit he'd never heard of them. Well, his current "significant" other had mentioned the big guy in the long black coat a few times but...should have paid more attention, he guessed. He was trying to sneak his two passengers/possible prisoners, through town without making a big deal of it. This was going to be a real circus for Branfield. As he had done every 10 minutes since he picked them up, he glanced at the back seat mirror and yes sir, there sat the two of them.

The tall guy still had his big black-brimmed hat pulled down over his eyes and wore the long black leather coat in spite of the summer temperature. The guy across from him, his manager, was much less mysterious in his blue tee shirt and jeans. Both were clean shaven. They both looked very pale and tired.

"What did I expect? The tall guy has been shot for God's Sakes and the other one apparently was his best friend! Not only that, but there were really big revelations coming when the other two cruisers got to the police station.

"How in the world could this city be in such a mess?" Jim Rollins asked himself out loud and then made a snap decision. "I need a bit of time here to think this through and give the town time to live with it.'

With that, he hit his radio and told his lead Captain that he was going to need a half hour or so to himself. He was going to drop his two passengers off at the station and wanted him to do the same. The people were to be put into separate interrogation rooms and told they would be questioned when their lawyers arrived. They were to be fed and given time to use the facilities. No one was to question them or talk to anyone about the happenings. Lt. Paul Davis was to see to it that each group was guarded at all times.

"I'll be back shortly." He said. "Stay cool and quiet about this."
He hit the OFF button and moved on down Oak Stet. Within a few minutes he sat in the small, tree-shaded park on the end of Elm St. where citizens were used to seeing him. He took a large gulp of his now cold coffee and allowed his mind to go back in time. Life for Branfield would never be the same, he thought. How in the world did this come to pass?

His ruminations began a few months ago...late winter or early spring...

HEARTLESS AMBITION

CHAPTER I

CHIEF JAMES ROLLINS

James Robert Rollins was born in Branfield, NH in the year 1958. His parents, Harry and Alice Rollins as well as his grandparents were well to do citizens of the little town. They were in the process of forming what was to become one of the leading home builders in New England and hoped their three children would follow in their footsteps. As often happens, none of their three children was interested in the building trade.

By the year 2022, their son Hal had become head curator of the local museum, Ann Louise had chosen to follow her calling and was a Catholic nun, and James had taken the office of Police Chief of their beloved town. Sadly, both of his parents, Harry Rollins and his wife, Alice, were deceased.

Harry and two others were the founders of ROLLINS INC., a home building company which was now being run very successfully by Kevin Samuel Clark, the son of an original partner and a founder of the company, Samuel Robert Clark. Sam Clark was still on the company's board as was Alex Douglas the third partner. All in the family had always been known to be fair, supportive in business and in helping with the town's growth. The town showed it. Schools were always graded in the excellent category; fiscal matters such as taxes were fair; the town was becoming more and more eclectic with the arrival of new workers anxious for their families to have an affordable place to live.

Chief James Robert Rollins had been their police chief for many years. It would be difficult for any citizen not to hope that he'd be there for many more. He had lost his wife far too early but had raised two children: Adam Howell, now 33, divorced and living in town and Virginia Ruth Grogan, now married and living in New Orleans.

On this day in early May, James had risen early, showered and decided to eat out. He took a last look in the hall mirror and announced to himself that breakfast at Betty's would be his first stop. His physique could afford a muffin or two. The workout at the gym was still paying off and at the age of 64 he looked damned good. All six feet plus of him was muscular and with a bit of help from Grecian Formula, his hair still gave him a year or two more. He had to admit the dark green of the uniform didn't do his ruddy complexion much good but all else was OK.

"Not bad, old man." Jim Rollins spoke aloud. "Now let's get on with Branfield's safety."

At eight AM, filled with gossip and muffins, he arrived at the station, greeted the force and made sure everything was in order. A few minutes later he began taking a cursory look at his mail. As usual, there didn't appear to be anything new in town that he would have to bother about.

He had done such a good job organizing the department that the town felt like that movie, *GROUNDHOG DAY* - nothing ever changed. His crew was well trained; their police cars always ordered every three years by the selectmen and shined daily by their drivers. Most citizens were proud of them and pleased with their own feeling of safety. His second in command, Lt. Davis, was quite capable of handling the work. What else did he have to do? This day, the whole thing was he felt no longer needed. Matter of fact, on May 12, 2022, he was bored to death.

The chief had been wondering lately if he should put his letter in the Mayor's box. He'd written it a month ago when his daughter up and left with her new husband. What a shock. One day she was always around the house and then, Wham! She had announced that she'd met the right man, would marry in January, and, that they would live in Louisiana.

Then his wayward son, Adam, had recently quit his job at ROLLINS INC. Then in a terse message he stated that he had left GERTZ HARDWARE. He had sent him a text, for God's Sakes. It announced that he might head off for greener pastures and not to worry. He promised to contact his father again as soon as he made some big decisions. The whole thing had left him feeling bereft and just a little afraid for his adventurous son. He'd always known the kids would grow up and vaguely that they might move away but never had considered it would come so soon.

"I'll be damned." He told Octavia in their morning routine call. "Is there no end to this? Did I do some really bad thing after their mother's death? Should I have spent more time with the two of them? I guess I had the time. This job as Chief of Police has been pretty tame. No real problems, a good bunch of people on my staff, a few domestic messes but this town is about as stable as those mountains up country."

"Face it, Jimmy. All youngsters want to try the world at some point. Are you worried about Adam? He's a big boy you know, in fact, a grown man. It's just that things change as the kids grow older. I say let's you and I just have a good time for once. Let the world take care of itself." Octavia answered brightly from her cell phone.

"Yeah, OK. I'll think about it. Right now, I've got to get the department going; get the new schedules up, and I'm planning on running around checking a few things. I shouldn't complain, I know, but this place does get pretty boring. I tell you what; let's find another place to have a drink this afternoon; not in Branfield. I need to see more of the world once in a while too, you know."

"No problem, Jimmy, I've just heard of a really nice spot. How about I make it a surprise." teased Octavia. "By the way, I think your idea about making friends and influencing people is really working. I can't tell you how many people Hal and I have met at the museum, who

3

mentions seeing you and your crew out and about regularly. They say it gives them confidence that their police force is aware and available; makes for a much happier and safer place to live in. Of course, I always make sure they understand that it was your idea, Jimmy."

Yeah, yeah." Jim answered. "You're just looking for a fancy meal. This place you're taking us to serve steak? OK, enough bantering. I'm off to patrol our metropolis."

With that, he gathered his gun from its safe, checked his uniform for looks, and headed off for another day, unaware that one of Branfield's biggest disasters was already in the works.

He would say later: "The problem that comes along in small towns is complacency. I can't count how often I have heard: 'Not in my town", when I've gabbed with the citizens about crime and political high jinx. I know better and want to say 'Don't get too confident. It's been my experience that small or large most of us live with the same positives and negatives; just less or more depending on the population. You never know what's going on right under your nose."

On the same day, Marion heard her phone jingle and for a minute thought of ignoring the thing. Who would be sending her texts at 8AM anyway? No doubt it would be some department store she'd visited or any one of the endless contacts she tried to block every day. Geez. She thought. I do like conveniences but this is becoming a nuisance. If it wasn't for the fact that Hal Rollins was so important in the town I'd probably go back to the tin cans and string Ma always joked about. The phone jingled again. She picked it up and checked to see. It was a text from Octavia. Probably on one of her crazy benders again she thought, then checked herself and couldn't resist. Who knows? Maybe this time it's important. The message read:

"Hold the presses! Strike up the band! Drag out the coffee! Yes, I know it's not Wednesday and probably you two are busy but, ladies, I have big news that'll shake us out of our doldrums. Is it possible that you could clear your schedules today and come for lunch?"

She tried to dismiss it, not really in the mood but still, she thought, maybe I should call Martha and see if she was up yet.

Martha was just relaxing and reviewing the past year or so as she refilled her coffee. Let's see, Dennis has been able to manage in the last year. How he had coped with the stress was beyond her but the hospital was still running. He was one of the doctors who had been asked to postpone all except life-saving surgeries and spend his time in the ER treating the huge influx of the flu's victims. He'd told her that he was glad he could help. As a result, he was exhausted all the time. She had tried to prepare meals that could be served at any odd time of the day, but even that hadn't really worked. Almost every day she had eaten alone after Dennis called to say he would bunk down at Rollins General. Octavia's message was still rolling round in her brain when the phone chimed.

She grabbed it and answered on the first ring. "Hi, Mare. I was just about to call you. What do you think? Is this Octavia being bored or something we need to hear?"

"Have we sunk so low that any news is welcome? That's a bit alarming. Perhaps it wouldn't hurt to investigate further. Also, it sounds as if she's stumbled on some news that might affect us or at least be interesting. As it happens I can be free and I'm curious today. What about you?" Marion said.

"You may be right, Marion. I know she and Hal have done wonders converting the old Rollins mansion into a museum and youth center. Along the way, I wonder if she's come upon some juicy town gossip or even a happening we might be interested in investigating." Martha mused.

"I don't know about the investigation bit but I guess I could cancel my hair thing. OK. Let's let her know and head for condo-land. How about around 11:30? I'll be glad to pick you up."

The call made, the two long-time friends mulled over what they expected. Would there be something that the town needed? Would whatever it was affect their life styles? Would this be just idle town gossip? They hadn't done so well investigating when Hal was in real trouble last year but they were wiser now...maybe this would be interesting.

Octavia was already opening the door when they reached for the buzzer.

"Wow. That was easy. How long has it been ladies? Too long whatever it is. We used to meet every Wednesday and I think those were some of the best times. I've been so damn bored some days. I'm hoping we'll come up with something new to do. I hate the pandemic but it is good that we three have been lucky." Olivia added. "In fact, wearing a mask indoors is still the norm here. Is that OK?"

"Of course." came immediately from Marion and Martha as they donned their masks.

By 12:30 the three were ensconced in Octavia's flowered lounge chairs enjoying the beautiful view from her glassed-in porch. The small river just across the street flowed quietly by offering up a wondrous reflection of puffy white cumulus against New Hampshire's brightest azure sky.

They devoured the delicious crab meat sandwiches, and got refills of iced tea then settled and Octavia began.

"So, yesterday, Hal and I were setting up a new exhibit when in comes Gladys Gertz of all people. We stopped our work and asked if we could help and she said she hoped so. Then she handed us a couple of posters. Would you believe she's running for mayor of Branfield? Gladys Gertz! She's been a great office manager and town clerk but...then she asked if we would be willing to put the posters up on our bulletin board and Hal said OK so I went along with it. Then I asked if she was planning on running against Andre and she announced that wouldn't be a problem because he was going to run for the state senate seat that Howard Brown had left. Well! Then, in that whispery voice she has, she asked if we'd be willing to donate money to both of their campaigns. We were both flummoxed. Hal said that we were a town run organization and didn't donate to specific candidates for office so off she went. What do you think of this turn of events?"

"You know what? I guess I haven't paid attention to the Gertz very much. Gladys was always very helpful if I needed a license or something but I know Hal has never been big time supportive of Andre.

He doesn't criticize much but once in a while he'd object to the way the town was being run and Andre was always right in the middle of whatever mayhem Hal suspected." Marion began.

"You're right, Mare." offered Martha. "This town has changed immensely since he became mayor. Even though the boys' place is going to make it as is, they often remark that they would like to find a way to help the average young couples be able to come in for a nice dinner once in a while. You know the population here used to be a much better mix of people than it is now...I wonder if that's to be laid at Mayor Andre Jan Gertz' feet?"

"You know what?" Octavia interjected. "I don't really know much about the Gertz story. If as you say, the town's changes have come since he took over, who's behind him? And, why don't we know?"

"Let's face it. It's got to be some people with money. I think Gladys agrees with the powers that be whoever they are and if Andre gets to be a senator I'd expect to see the whole state going to the rich as well. Not my cup of tea." said Marion.

The three nursed their curiosity silently while they devoured the macaroons Octavia produced.

Marion spoke first. "Have the Gertz always been in this town? How did he make such a success of his life? And why would Gladys have been the one he chose for his wife?"

"I'd say do we really care?" added Octavia. "If I do, why do I care?"

"My answer is yes." said Martha. "I care because this has always been my town; my state for that matter and I see so much change here that I feel I should know more. Let's face it we have time and in the long run might just come up with some ideas to help our town." She added in afterthought.

"Well, I have made it a rule to share stuff with Hal. Lord knows, it would have saved a lot of heartache for him if his family had done so last year. I don't think he'll object as long as we stick to the idea of

7

helping Branfield. He's very proud of our town. So I'll be glad to be involved if you want me to." said Marion.

"OK, then. If it's alright with you two I suggest we make a list of what we want to know and put some time in. We could then report next week on Wednesday and see what we have." Martha put in.

"I'm game," Said Octavia enthusiastically. "And I have a friend who knows a lot of inside info. This could be just the thing for us to get us back into life again." She hesitated and then went on, "Just in case this was what we decided, I have printed up a few of the things I think I'd like to know. Take a look."

She passed out a folder to her two friends and then added. "Read this stuff over and let me know if you would prefer one idea or another to look into and I'll make a better list of it. This could be fun."

Marion and Martha immediately took the time to read Octavia's ideas.

"Well, well. Who would believe we're thinking of taking some responsibility for our town?" said Marion. "Probably we should have been paying more attention much earlier but what the heck. I like what you've done Tavia. If Martha thinks it's OK, I'd be glad to do the history of the Gertz family. I still have quite a few sources I can tap from my teaching stuff. And, I have boxes of my mom's stuff I haven't had the courage to go through. It's hard to believe both Ma and Dad are gone..." Her voice trailed off.

"Damn. Time does march on ladies. So let's see if we want to become political and get involved with Andre Jan Gertz." Martha stated. "I can mush around and find out what I can about how the town is run and who the real movers and shakers are. Do you still stay in contact with Jim Rollins, Octavia? He should be a fountain of info."

"That's my other news." She said with a big smile. "Jimmy and I have decided to give it another try. You know neither of us has been happy since we called it off, so we're going to make things better. I think I really love the guy. I've decided who cares if he has this wayward son?"

"I agree with you choice." said Marion. "I've been really impressed with the way he's kept the police department going in this town. I'm assuming the fact that he has one or two officers walking a beat on some of our main streets and that he's out cruising the whole town every day himself, is his way of keeping us all safe and happy. Sure has been a pleasant change from the old days when we all felt we had to hide or look the other way at the sight of a cop. I just saw his car go by this morning, it's kind of nice to know he's around."

The three old friends spent another hour wishing Octavia luck while they basked in the sun. They agreed to meet just to gossip in one week and in two weeks they planned on being ready to discuss their research to find out the who's and what's of Andre Jan Gertz and his wife, Gladys Medford Gertz.

CHAPTER II

GOING STRONG

'Welcome, welcome. How did May 18 get here so fast? "Come on in and let's see what our worlds are all about." Olivia offered as she opened the door.

"If that's all you want to know I can tell you. I'm bored, vacant brained, and getting fatter by the minute. Could it be I'm finally past the point of no return?" offered Marion. "I don't even know what has happened to the last 7 days never mind a year plus. It's so hard to believe that we're in the second year of this stuff. I don't think I've missed anything more than our meetings."

"I agree totally." interjected Martha. "Dennis has been used and abused and I still see people ranting about wearing a mask, and Dr. Fauci is always being questioned as if he were Hitler or some other criminal. What in the world is happening here?"

"Oh come on you broads. So we've had to cope with a few little inconveniences for a while. I know for a fact that you two have lived through worse things. Remember the year your son-in-law, Jason, had that odd cancer, Marion? You led the whole family through the awful thing. And, look at you, Martha. I know we're all beating the door on number 70, but no one would bet on it when they see you. Have you got any idea how much I'd like to put on a bathing suit like yours? Bathing suit? HAH! Even a pair of those stretchy pants that are all the rage...maybe even a Mumu..."

"Please, Olivia. You haven't changed a bit; still off to never, never land at the drop of an idea." Marion interrupted. "How lucky could three old broads be? Here we are flourishing! I'll bet each of us knows someone who has an acquaintance who didn't make it alive. Hal's cousin Rachael for example. One day she was over visiting him and she even had a mask on but Wham! Within 4 days Al called and said she was on a ventilator. She didn't make it, you know, and she was only 50. I think we've done the right thing holing up for a few months."

"I'm thinking it may be quite a few more months until we beat this thing. Listen up, let's pretend just for today. We've been good and none of us has gotten sick. It's time to grab our masks and venture down to a store...there must be one without many customers...Ah the thrill of it all...imagine touching real, new, t-shirts; or maybe even a frilly top with sequins...Matter-of-fact, I've been hankering for a hot fudge sundae. *ANNA'S* is calling and that's outdoors." Marion's countenance grew calmer with each word.

"Ice cream, maybe, but where could we go if we bought something new?" said Martha. "My boy's restaurant is barely scraping by and if it wasn't for the fact that the damn virus kept Dennis working 12-15 hour shifts, we'd probably be close to financial ruin. Go? Have either of you had your vaccine?" As she looked around she realized her error and added, "Of course you have. Let's be realistic, friends. Maybe we could take a walk up the cliff out here but..."

"You're a damn spoil sport Marth; just too grounded, as they say. Let me think. Ok, let's just gossip." offered Marion.

"Well, wait a minute." Octavia said. "I'd like to catch up with just living for a few seconds. Is there anything we've not talked about since our meeting last week? Anybody die we know about? How about a new TV show? Darn sure no one in our crew would be having a baby or graduating, or...”

“Oh, I know.” Marion piped up. “We had kind of an interesting thing happen this week; with the youngest granddaughter Jackie. Maybe it would give us hope at least. I’ll tell you what, she’s sure is smart for a 7 year old. I have to admit she came along as a big surprise but she’s been just the firecracker we needed; happy, always thinking of others. I bet none of us could hold a candle. Anyway I think you’d be fascinated with Angie’s tale.”

With positive nods, her two friends settled into their rockers.

Marion hurried on: “This is the story she told. Let’s see...I’m going to attempt to remember her exact words:

“Nana, Wait ’til you hear what happened to me. Listen up now. It was last Monday and it was time. I had planned this for days. It was 7AM. I opened my eyes to see if everything I had planned was still OK. Yes. My piggy bank sat exactly where I had left it and the apple fritter I hadn’t finished lay on the sill. Suddenly I realized that the sunlight was coming through the blinds. I jumped out of bed. The whole thing was going to be awful if I didn’t move quickly. It seemed as if the clock must have been greased. Gee Whiz! Was I going to be able to get out without him noticing?

“By the smell of bacon coming up the stairs, I knew I would have to hurry if I was to get back and give it to him with breakfast. I stuffed my little bank and my tablet in its case ready to be grabbed and tip-toed down the back stairs and walked to the store two blocks away.

“Hey. Ms. Grafton.” I said as I entered the Walgreen’s. “I need a big birthday card for my dad. He is very old, 35 today, and I think I have just enough saved.” With that I stood at the counter, opened my tablet and found the page I needed. Right in the middle was the card with the big red truck on the cover. The driver looked a little like my dad and there was a kid I liked to think was me, sitting up front next to him. There was a big black 35 on the door-it was the best card ever. Ms. Grafton said she knew just where the card was and found it in a minute. Then she rang up the cost.

13

"*'That will be four dollars and 36 cents.' She said. 'That's what I thought.' I said and then I turned the bank up-side down. Nothing! No pennies. No dimes. None of the quarters Grampa had stuffed into my pocket each time he visited. I wanted to cry. No time to find out who had raided my bank, but I bet it was that 13 year old Jake, my brother, that did it. My heart was broken. My plan wouldn't work. I couldn't stop the tears. What would I tell dad?*

"*Suddenly, beside me I heard a man's voice. 'What a wonderful present for you to give to your dad.' He said. I blew my nose and turned around. I had not even noticed the tall man waiting behind me with his morning coffee and donut. 'I tell you what. I'll lend you the money for the card and you can pay me back whenever you want. Please, Ms. Grafton, just ring this up with my things.' I wanted to thank him but when I stopped crying he was gone. Besides, I needed to go. I ran home with my gift.*

"*A little way down the sidewalk to our house I saw all kinds of excitement. There was a police car in our driveway! People were running around looking up and down the street. Wow! I thought. Dad must have caught Jake with my piggy bank money. Brat! Then everything turned around. Dad came running down the block and hugged and kissed me. The police came right behind him asking if I was OK. Even Jake looked concerned. What in the world? Did they already know about the beautiful card? In an instant, Dad began:*

"*'Where have you been? Why did you go out without telling us? You're in big trouble, young lady.'*"

"The harangues continued forever, it seemed." Martha continued the story.

"And obviously, she said she, not Jake, was the one who had done wrong. She said she did get to give her dad his card and try to explain. She said that the day didn't seem much fun but Dad and Momma finally gave her a kiss and a lot of hugs so she guessed everything was alright now.

I asked her if she learned anything that day and I have to say she hit the nail on the head." said Marion as she paused to recall. "Now don't forget she's only 7." She said:"

'It doesn't take much to get into real trouble. Good intentions don't really matter either. But sometimes somebody nice comes along and makes everything just good. I hope I'll be kind someday too.'

"I asked her if she had ever seen that man before that morning and she said no. Then I asked if she could describe him. The only thing I got was that he wore a long black coat and had thick glasses on. She said his voice was very soft and he had a big hat that covered his eyes. I'm guessing that could mean it had a wide brim, maybe. I couldn't get any real idea of his age. She did say maybe he was a little older than her dad.

"OK that's my story. Do any of you know a pretty tall guy who wears a long black coat in our town???" Marion said as she finished her contribution.

"Well, in the first place, I don't think it's any big deal if a kind man helps out a little girl in broad daylight. Are you thinking there was something odd about that?" offered Octavia. "It's sure is a messy world that can't accept the graciousness of a human being toward another. There were many times in my life when I could have used a helping hand. Is this one of our "not in my town' things?"

"I admit I've been lucky to have found Dennis." Martha added. "He's pretty good at knowing when I'm in great distress. Distress, now that's an interesting word. Here we have a little girl burdened with it. Geez! What would so many of us do right now without the CDC or our president or the many others who work so hard each day to keep us calm...not only calm but in many cases fed and cared for. This is a colossally difficult time in our lives... all of us could use a tall man in a wide brimmed hat..."

"Martha. Martha. For goodness sakes, I didn't mean to set you off. This was just a passing story and to be honest, I was wondering about this man. This is still a smallish place and I can't believe I wouldn't know practically everyone."

15

"For God's sake you two; let's get back to the shopping suggestion." muttered Octavia. "It's May 2022. We've been good for over a year and we've all gotten the 2 shots. I vote yes. Let's put on our shopping garb and get at it. I know you're still a newlywed, Marion, so is Hal coming home soon? Or can we just hit the mall for a couple of hours. I have a brand new mask I want you to see. Besides, maybe we'll get ice cream too. To hell with COVID19! Viva our vaccinations! Let's go!" And with that Octavia led the trio out the door. A couple of hours later, the three old friends had pitched their newly purchased items under their feet and sat chattering over hot fudge at ANNA'S outside table.

"OK." offered Octavia. "We've done it. We've exited our caves and made some attempt at rejoining society. So far, I don't see either of you turning green with the flu so ...what now?"

"First, I think we still need to keep guard on our safety." added Marion. "I don't plan on throwing my masks away just yet. You know the DELTA strain is still around. That could do us in."

"My God! Mare. Leave it to you to be practical on such a great day." interrupted her friend. "I'm happy as a lark to have that new scarf and I'll bet the good doctor will be ecstatic when that blue lacy thing makes an appearance tonight. It was fun, Marion. She glanced over at Octavia and was startled by the look on her face. What's the matter, Octave, seen a ghost?"

"I don't think so but still...I think I just saw the mystery man going down the sidewalk. Did either of you notice? He was kind of strolling towards an older Toyota. Seemed tall and had a black wide brim... wonder who he is... I felt as if I had seen him before..."

"There could be a new person in town, you know." said Marion. "Hey. It's getting late; time to get home. I've had a wondrous time."

"No, no, no. you two, don't forget what we were planning. I've told Jimmy that I'd share whatever I found, is that OK?" Octavia piped up.

"No problem here." Marion offered in a hurry. "I almost forgot and I have a bunch of info; how about you, Marth?"

"Well I must say I found the life and times of Andre and Gladys Gertz quite interesting; Better than my mundane existence."

At that point, Marion and Martha snapped to and each presented Octavia with a folder filled with information.

"OK. So, what do we now know about our mayor? And do we care?" said Octavia as she glanced through the pages.

"I tell you what. Why don't you both package up your info and send it to me. Then give me a week and I'll piece it together so that we'll be able to just read what we've found." interjected Marion. "I know you are busy at the museum, Octave, and obviously Dennis and your kids are your first concern Marth, so I have time on my hands and plenty of computer paper just hanging around. I can probably see to it that next week we'll have a book to read."

All agreed with that then hopped into Marion's Accord and headed home.

CHAPTER III

THE WOMEN AND THE GERTZ

A week after their meeting at Octavia's, Marion's doorbell rang. She couldn't have been more surprised. There stood the postal carrier announcing she had two special-delivery packages and would need her signature to receive them.

"Hello Mary. Are you sure these are for me and not Hal? I think this is the first special-delivery I've ever gotten."

"Oh yes, Marion. As you know the USPS is doing its best to keep people safe and still informed so we're making more home delivery if we can. This is kind of out of the way, but it's nice to see you again."

"OK. Many thanks and where do I sign? Be careful on these mountain roads, now."

Both of the over-sized letters were marked PRIORITY MAIL. One was from Octavia and the other Martha. Even though she had planned a big cleaning of the house she couldn't resist and went directly to the kitchen, made a new pot of coffee and headed for the den. It took no time at all to see that these were their research efforts as to Branfield and the Gertz.

As expected, Martha had taken the time to record her information in outline form making sure to add in red type each person to whom she had spoken while Octavia's was hand written and had many personal opinions jotted throughout. She settled down reading and re-reading what they had found. Finally, she felt she could condense the whole thing. After four days she had liberally used their personal notes and had a reasonable book-like form that would make it easy when they met. She hoped they would agree with her interpretation. The work read as follows:

ANDRE AND GLADYS GERTZ

It was January 19, 2017 and Gustave Eric Gertz, a local Language professor in Lieige, Belgium, was antsy. He had a new wife and they wanted a family. Daily, he had stood up to his relatives in Liege, telling them that he wanted, no needed, a change. What he made as a part time teacher was nowhere near what they needed to survive. That was partially true but in fact, as a well-read, educated man, he was alarmed at the dark political clouds hanging over Europe. WWI had begun for most of Europe in 1914.

His beloved country, Belgium, had declared itself neutral in the European melee with Germany. Still, it looked as if they would have to get involved. Germany was strong and invading many of the countries surrounding it. He knew that trouble was on the horizon. His country's leaders were even in the process of drafting an army. He could not face the possibility that even at 26 years old he would be drafted. There was no way he wanted that for his future children.

Even though the United States had thrown in their army in April of 1917, America's distance from the war made it seem much safer than Europe. America's opportunities made a loud call and he and his wife

Maude, proceeded to discuss the move immediately. He was surprised at how quickly she encouraged the change, but as he thought about it she had always been his strongest supporter.

Once they agreed the real hassle began. The questions were many: Would their parents wish to join them? Would they be allowed to leave? Was there any boat transportation for emigrants? What did they need for paperwork? Where were they going to live? What town would they like? Would Gustave be able to support his family there? Doing what? What should they take with them? What would all of this cost? As was his want, he took them one at a time.

The first was not easy. It was soon obvious that neither set of parents were prepared to make such a change. They said they would be devastated at their children's departure but felt too old to try such a major undertaking. Sadness fell over the two families but the courage of youth prevailed and Maude and Gustave vowed they must go.

As for the second problem: Where would they go? Given the fact that he was grateful for his wife's willingness to go at all, he immediately suggested that they should try the same place her cousin and best friend had chosen. He then assigned Maude to dig out their old maps of the United States and copy down all information. Within a week Maude had gotten a detailed description of what she now considered her own little town, Branfield, New Hampshire. He knew that the climate was similar to theirs, how many people lived in the town, and that there were other immigrants there who could give them advice. It was perfect, she told him.

The third question was soon solved. Maude had a distant cousin who had made the change and in correspondence extolled the life they had found in Branfield, New Hampshire. They told them that they had been able to get passage from the Norwegian port of Oslo to New York. It hadn't been easy but because Norway had declared itself a neutral country as well, they had been able to secure passage with the help of a politician in Liege. Maybe they could do the same.

The fourth hurdle was harder. There was some question as to whether or not Gustave's credentials would be good enough so that he could get a university job in the new world. Once again, Maude came up with a solution. To make ends meet in Belgium, Gustave had been helping his father deliver milk, cheese, and other farm products to Liege citizens for the last five years. She suggested that he could make a good living by establishing a regular similar route, and also suggested he add an "unwanted items" pick-up schedule for their new town.

"You're personable and at ease with hard work. You have a knack for carpentry, and an eye for a bargain. I'm sure you could start a new business in Branfield." She said. "Perhaps later on you would be able to go back to teaching but I think you need to see a sure way to support our venture."

"I've got other good news." added Maude. "Cousin Alicia has written that Peter has seen a ten acre piece of land just on the outskirts of town that would be ideal for a family. He said he knew Gustave was clever and would be able to expand on the home that was already there as well as keep a garden and pasture for the horses necessary to pull his supply wagon. As for work, he said the town was growing very fast and certainly needed someone to handle delivery of produce and the idea of picking up their flotsam could work well. He said that most people just burned household leftovers but in order to be a real town they needed to change their ways. It was possible that the town would be willing to hire someone industrious like Gustave to create a pick up route and that they would probably be happy to allow him to establish some kind of "odds and ends" shop on his property. He also mentioned that there were many horse-less cars now being manufactured in America. In fact, he already had ordered one from FORD. That might be a better choice than oxen or horses, but that the little farm would support whatever he chose.

"Maybe that would be a better choice." said Maude. "Guess what? You might just be a needed part of the town's government."

"Wow! Maude. You surely think way ahead. Who would have thought that a little teacher from Belgium could think about being a king in America? Only you. Maybe it will come true but first, we must get there so let's do our planning now."

As for other immigrants, there was no problem. Whatever news Gustave could find always said that America was a big country and they welcomed anyone who would help make it successful.

"It sounds like any town will be grateful for new citizens like us. I say let's put it into the works." said Gustave with the enthusiasm of youth. "You've done a great job with our planning. Do you know how much I love you and rely on you?" he said to Maude with a big hug. "You are my rock, my dear; I wouldn't be anything without you."

"Thank you, Gustave, but I'm sure you'd have done very well without me." Maude teased.

The last and probably the most important task was to take a close look at their finances. They had been married for a year and a half and had tried very hard to pinch pennies as they set up housekeeping. Aside from groceries and the books Gustave brought home from the book store each week, they had managed not to spend any extra and as a result now had saved a few hundred dollars.

Within a week they discovered that there would be minimal ticket money needed for the train to Oslo; about $2, but because of the exodus from Europe and Norway's willingness to make the treacherous cruise to New York, the prices had been rising constantly. They decided they would be alright if they went in second or third cabin status. In Third Class, the price for two was $100, and would include two trunks. With the enthusiasm and adventurous spirit of the young, they added the small amount Maude's parents offered and booked their passage for April 12. It would take 4-6 days to make the trip depending on the possibility that they might have to adjust the trip to avoid German submarines.

Europe was now in a full-fledged war; it was time to go. On Tuesday, April 12, 1917, the day of their departure, they now had $1500 left to set up their future. Maude and Gustave hugged each other for strength and worked for the next two weeks getting their affairs in order.

The Gertz arrived on April 21 of 2017. He was 27 and she, 19. They had been lucky not to have been hit by the German subs patrolling the Atlantic. It had been a hassle getting through customs at Ellis Island

23

but within a day they had found a train to New Hampshire. Maude's second cousin, Alicia and her husband Peter met them in the city of Portsmouth. There were hugs and handshakes all around-a welcoming sight for the weary couple.

As many others had done before them, they looked in wonder at their new world. The docks near the train depot were alive with uniformed American soldiers. Some were leaving while many others greeted their families through bandages, tears and lost limbs.

"My God!" Gustave whispered to Maude. "What a sacrifice these people have made for the world. I will see to it that I thank them because without their help I fear Europe will be doomed."

Gustave admired the number of horse driven carriages and work wagons hauled by oxen. He would fit right in, he thought. He was more in wonder as he saw the few but fascinating motor cars. FORD seemed to be the most popular name.

The town of Branfield was smaller than he had imagined. Peter took them down the main street on the way to see their new home. Liège had had many streets of that size and many shops and businesses along the way. Branfield seemed to be made up of three main streets with two-story colonial homes on each side. He was impressed by the river running through the center of town; it would certainly give the area power for a factory or two. Within a mile of their Main Street, the buildings were surrounded by 3-10 acre farms, all with large barns. Less than a mile later, Peter suddenly parked his new Model A. There directly ahead was a wooden gate guarding a winding gravel road through rows of newly budding maples.

"Oh my goodness!" Maude spoke in awe. "Is this the area you think we can afford, Peter?"

"Yup. This is 593 Pine Street, Branfield, NH." He answered. "Land is still pretty cheap in this country. Don't forget it's around three thousand miles wide; very different from out little Belgium."

"Let's take a look at what we have. I can't wait one more minute." Gustave was chomping at the bit.

"OK. Here we go." said Peter as he cranked the car's motor over. "This is the main gate and there's about a quarter mile lead in to the house."

It was obvious that New Hampshire was still dealing with the rough winters of the area. Their entry road was rutted and muddy but Gustave could see a few red or green sprouts on each side indicating spring was on the way. The raw eastern breezes kept the temperature in the low 50's but they were so excited to finally be in this spot they hardly noticed. Soon they saw the wide fields to right and left and suddenly the small home and barn.

"This will be ours, Maude. Can we make it here?" Gustav whispered.

"It will be our palace when we're done," she answered as she squeezed her husband's hand. "It couldn't be better."

"Peter, how much acreage did you say would go with this home?" said Gustave.

"It's approximately ten." He answered. "And, I understand the owners as anxious to sell. I've been told it can be bought for five hundred. Is that within your budget?"

"Oh, yes. We're certainly not rich but I'm sure we can make a go of it here. As far as the house goes, let's take a look. Do you have permission to go in?"

"Yes. I have the key but I'll bet it's open anyway. There aren't many people here who lock their doors at night. They're a trusting bunch."

The house was as expected. No one had lived in it for a year and dust had taken over. The mustiness of neglect caused each of them to grimace and then sneeze. The owners had taken everything they wanted and left a great deal of furniture. Most of it was very used and Gustave didn't see how he could repair it. The living room windows had heavy woven curtains, once a bright maroon but faded gray. The kitchen contained a black iron wood stove whose chimney rose at a dangerous angle and the small wooden table showed the signs of many years of chopping vegetables for canning. Gustave was unsure. Maybe they had made a mistake.

But with one look around, Maude smiled and took over. She loved the two 6-pane windows on either side of the front door. The house had a built in room inside with a toilet and a sink fed by a hand pump. The kitchen sported a hand pump, and four cabinets, two up and two down. She could dress it up with a bit of elbow grease.

"No problem," she said. "Just a bit of sewing and maybe some paint and you'll be surprised. It doesn't look as if the ceilings have leaked. I don't see one stain. My mother taught all of us girls to sew and clean. I can't wait to begin."

Gustave was bowled over. He had had no idea that he was marrying such an adventurous and capable woman when they tied the knot.

After they had inspected the three bedrooms upstairs, they headed for the barn to see what they had there. It was small but full of promise. There were stalls for five or six animals. Horses? Oxen? A cow? And room outside for a chicken coop. This far from the center of town had no municipal water supply so there was a dug well which looked adequate as well. He had expected to see an outhouse but that was one more positive thing they had already discovered.

"Gustave, Gustave. We have found our home. I think we should make an offer today and get started. The few things we have had sent by cargo ship are due to arrive in a month and I'd like our mansion to be up to snuff by then." Maude said gleefully.

"You make the whole adventure worth it, my love." He whispered as he held her close. "You're right. America will be our life- we will make it so."

Still, the boys at HERM'S BAR felt the need to investigate and see if they should be welcomed. They made every effort, stopping people on the street, inquiring about real estate deals in town, and quizzing their kids each day after school. It paid off and in a couple of weeks they were able to discuss the conversational dossier that resulted. The first piece of information came from their friend, the blacksmith.

He knew the new people. They were acquainted with his wife. He had helped them with their trip. That was enough. Then they learned that they came from Belgium and this info shot that to the top of their list.

Most were fascinated. Belgium?! Who knew anyone from that country? Where was it anyway? They heard that they spoke French there for goodness sakes-that should be France shouldn't it? Henry Boudoin, a carpenter from Canada, met the couple and was bowled over that they could speak French and English equally well. Eventually one of the diner's regulars who had relatives in Belgium set them straight. Lots of people in Belgium spoke French and many spoke Dutch, he announced and all was right with their world again. It wasn't long before all of the townies knew that there was a man named Gustave and his wife Maude who had arrived in town in 1917. They spoke French or English and they seemed resourceful and ordinary-their importance to their discussions waned. Maude and Gustave paid little attention to the curiosity of the town. They were just too busy getting their home livable and self-supporting.

There were five or six neighbors near the Gertz farm and all had been a bit curious when they visited and discovered the many books that had come in one of the trunks they had seen unloaded. It almost seemed as if there were enough to fill their little library.

"Where did they come from?" They asked. "Was Gustave some kind of elite in Belgium? Could it have been Maude's family that came from another class?"

As a consequence of their curiosity, these women made it a goal to get to know Maude. On the first quick coffee and gossip session, Maude set the mystery at bay.

"No. No. It was just that his father was a milk and cheese delivery man. His mother loved to learn and instilled education into their only son. By the time he was 20, Gus was accepted as an instructor in one of Liege's public schools." She added. "He really enjoyed teaching but it wouldn't pay enough to support a growing family. I hope someday he'll be able to get back to it."

27

The coffee klatch crew made sure to swap the information at the supper table and with that, the Gertz family was welcomed into the town.

Along the way many neighbors offered furniture they no longer needed and when electricity came to most of the town's center, the local feed and grain store had been happy to sell them one of the new refrigerators that had just come in. With care and feeding, the big stove already in the kitchen now gleamed and the red pump had been replaced by an electric pump connected to their well.

Soon, the routine of farming and survival set in. Gustave began his daily trek through the settled parts of town, offering to take their unwanted goods and furniture away for a small price. The gossip couldn't be contained. They'd all seen his wagon and the matched set of draft horses, of course, so that passed their interest, but wasn't he a bit overdressed? Who was this man in the newly pressed black suit, his white shirt and tie front and center? No one in Branfield, New Hampshire had ever heard of such a thing! They had always thought that one's first appearance mattered. In this case, it made Gustave feel as good as anyone else; maybe even a bit better as he got to express his individuality. Maude smiled as she ironed tomorrow's shirt.

Suit and tie or not, it was quite an enterprising man they saw each week. He made it his job to comb the neighborhoods for things they no longer wanted. Sometimes people just sat them out near the side of the street and once in a while he just spied their unwanted stuff in their backyard or piled up behind a shed and asked if they would like him to just take it away. Occasionally, he'd offer a bit of change for their castoffs but more often they were just glad to see it go. What luck, they thought. Normally they would just toss old stuff in to a pile in the back woods or yard, and then burn it when winter came. What in the world was he going to do with the stuff?! Gustave and Maude just smiled to themselves. She knew what he'd do with things he found. It paid the bills.

Within a year, because of their actions, Gustave and Maude Gertz were accepted as citizens. They seemed nice enough; kept to themselves and went to church too. That made everything Ok. As a matter of fact, they liked knowing that someone was around who was going to come by with his horse-driven wagon like clockwork every week and be willing to collect any of the things they no longer needed in their lives.

People weren't even too shocked when Gustave opened a small thrift shop in the front half of his barn. He used it to display the things he had collected and repaired and his prices were kept at a minimum. Some of the elite in town made quiet objections to his opening what they thought of as "a junk shop", but even many of them were glad to know that there was a place where they might find that replacement wheel for their buggy, or a bureau needed for the baby's room, or maybe even a set of dishes that would do for just starting out. What difference would it make if a cup or saucer was missing? As time marched on, the offerings at Gus's emporium moved with it. It was often the place where one could find engines, steering wheels, or most automobile parts. It was impressive what he could repair and or refurbish, then offer to sell for a reasonable sum. In fact, in just a few short years, this Belgium fellow became the most popular entrepreneur in their town.

The Gertz family soon had two daughters, Hilda, born in 1930, and Mildred in 1932. By then, Gustave had bought a cow, a dozen chickens, a matched pair of draft horses, and Maude had seen to it that they had a garden planted. They had a thriving business, food and a home to be proud of

When Maude approached her early 40's she confided in some of the neighborhood women that she and Gustave were considering having another baby. Many of the women cautioned Maude that this was a dangerous age to have a child but Maude and Gus had still decided to give it one more try.

ANDRE JAN GERTZ AND HIS SURROGATES

The world is not always kind, however, and tragedy struck them. On October 12, 1945, Maude died from complications while giving birth to their only son, Andre Jan Gertz. Gustave was devastated. So much so that Hildy and Millie now 15 and 17, had no one to care about them for months. The town was sympathetic, bringing casseroles and tears, but soon the concern waned and they went back to their own worries. All agreed that things would work out OK in the long run.

Days became nearly a year and the little home filled with memories that kept Gustav unable to work. In fact it was a neighbor who checked in each day to see if the girls were alright. Sometimes she took time to show them how to do at least basic cleaning. But, it was obvious that the problems of caring for a small baby were overwhelming to both the girls and their father. In addition, money became an issue and Gustav knew he needed to get back to his weekly runs. The family needed to be supported. Knowing and doing became his biggest burden. He just couldn't seem to do more than get up each day never mind make plans for the future.

Lucky for Gustave, Ella Cranston and her husband Wilbur lived a half mile or so away and in August of '46, she made a visit to Gustave's. Nothing was as she hoped.

"My God. If depression could make a noise the house would have rivaled living on a train track." She repeated to Wilbur that evening. "You wouldn't believe what Gus is asking of those two young girls. I would say they do any housework that is done and let me tell you that's very little. I saw unmade beds, soiled diapers thrown in corners, dishes piled in the sink, at least a few days' worth. It was overwhelming! I don't have any idea what the girls wear to school but I don't think the ones they had on had been touched by water for weeks. They're old enough but don't seem to be able to take charge and let me tell you..."

"Listen, Ella, is this any of your business?" Wilbur interrupted. "I'd say it was nice of you to visit but...I don't know I'm trying to imagine what I'd be thinking if I had a busy body seeing my downfall...I don't know..."

"Oh, for goodness sakes, Wilbur, I'm just reporting to you. I have no intention of publishing my findings in the local paper! Sometimes you make me feel so..." she obviously searched for a word. "Untrustworthy, I guess. I really did go over there just to offer my help but...this was so beyond that. I. No. I'm not apologizing. What I'm saying is that that family next door is not going to make it another month without some aid." With that she left the room and ruminated for the afternoon.

By the following week, she contacted friends in the near vicinity and invited them to her home for an afternoon of tea, cake and planning. At 2pm, she met Edna Hamden, Doris Plant, Susan Elliot, and Nancy Hall at the door with a hug. After a few inquiries as to each of their family's health and well-being, Ella settled down and began.

"Thanks for coming. I'm hoping you won't think I'm a busy body but there's a problem here that I think needs attention." Her friends ceased their chattering. They were intrigued.

"What's going on, Ella? Is someone ill? Is Will OK?" They all spoke at once.

"Well, yes and no. But come on in to the parlor and help yourselves to some tea. Those things you see on the table were supposed to be petit fours, 'fit for one's best formal dinners' *GOOD HOUSEKEEPING* said last month. Somehow I think I failed the directions. I did taste one though and it was really good. Maybe just close your eyes and go for it. Then let's sit and I have a proposition for us." Ella said getting to the point in a hurry.

"As you know, Maude Gertz passed away nearly 10 months ago. I didn't know her well, but she was really pleasant the last time I saw her, maybe when she was about 8 months along. She had done miracles for that house you know, making it so cozy and bright. The Walshes would be amazed at what can be done when you try. Have any of you seen the place?"

Susan spoke first. "I was over there probably at the end of September. I wanted to see if Gus could pick up that brown couch we have in the front room. Oh by the way, he likes to be called Gus now.

31

She was busy but took time to offer a glass of ice water and we had a nice chat. She was probably seven months along and said this had been her most difficult pregnancy. They were hoping for a boy of course but whatever it was, it going to be her last, she said."

"Yes, the men always want a son, don't they?" muttered Doris. "I think Jack would insist on trying again if we hadn't had the two boys right away."

"You sure are right, Sue." chimed in Nancy. "We've got five of the little devils and I wouldn't want any more."

"Oh, for goodness sakes," said Edna. "Mark and I can't seem to produce even one of any kind. You ladies don't know how hard that is!"

"Darn. I'd say this is a great conversation for another day." Ella interrupted. "We've got quite an age group here. Doris, you must be about my age. Lord knows, Ken and I are glad to have our two girls married and settled. And I'd guess you're still not forty, Susan. Edna, I wouldn't make a try at your age. You never seem to age to me. Anyway, our different ages should provide some good ideas among us. Kids are what I want to talk about with all of you. As you know, Gus and his girls are trying to take care of little Andre over there. Those girls are 15 and 17 you know and Andre is just about four months. I've gone over a few times to try to show them what to do but...well Gus is so depressed. He can't seem to pull himself together at all. I was wondering if our group here could help.

"Forgive me if I'm off- base here but, are any of you working, or obligated too much to allow you to put in some time? My thoughts were that we could take turns, maybe a couple of days every week and just take care of little Andre until things settle over there. Oops, my mistake. You're so quiet, Nancy, I forgot to ask you. Where do you fit in this bunch? You can't be a day over 30, am I right?"

"Wow! I like that. No I'm about to hit 50 but I do appreciate the flattery." said Nancy.

"Well, good for you. So, that makes five of us. We could even just promise one day. What do you think?"

"Wow!" Edna spoke first. "I confess. I'm fifty one and just want to work a few more years. I'm not working right now but I've been offered a position at Rollins. I'd just decided to accept the other day. So I guess I'd be out. I'd be glad to babysit once in a while if necessary."

"Congrats, Edna. I know you.ve been looking. Will you be some kind of executive?" asked Nancy.

"No, I'm afraid not. This bunch is modern, I think, but not when it comes to a woman executive. We'll see. We women have got the vote now you know and that may make a difference."

"Well, let's see." Nancy came back. "I think the best solution would be for Gus to hire someone to housekeep and be there during the day. Then maybe if it became necessary, he could feel free to call on one of us to babysit on an evening. He's been at his collection business for quite a while now so I bet his savings are running out. If we could get him back to work it would be good for him and he could afford it. I'm working over at the library now so I could easily find some estimates as to the salary we could suggest. I can let you know, probably by tomorrow. By the way, would one of us want to take it over?"

"Gosh. I hadn't even considered that, Nance. It might very well be something I'd like." Doris said thoughtfully. "Maybe Gus wouldn't want that, though. Plus, I'd have to discuss it with Jack. Our John has just decided to join the US navy and Ham is off to Boston College in the fall; we're rattling around the place alone. I guess it would be possible to handle it just until the girls were home from school and settled. I don't know...let me think about it and we can approach him."

"If I were Gus, I'd jump right on that offer." said Susan. "What do you suppose that kind of arrangement would be worth? Are you sure you don't want to go back to work? I thought you were interested in heading up the school cafeteria crew?"

"No. I'm not in the mood to go back there. Jack has been out of work since the crash you know and we think that this job for me would give him more time to find something good. It shouldn't be too hard and I'm hoping I can count on all of you to help if I get buried. Of course, we haven't even discussed this with Gus so who knows, he might not want to do this."

"I tell you what. If it's OK with you and Jack, Doris, why don't I contact him tomorrow and if he's interested we'll go over there next Saturday. In the meantime, do a bit of digging Nancy. Let's have some kind of figure to offer."

All agreed and after another cup of tea they left for home.

They had decided to approach the situation with honesty and compassion accepting whatever they found without reaction. A much disheveled Gustave opened the door at their knock and invited them in without apologies. His ever-present shirt and tie were obviously in need of care. "Good afternoon, ladies." He mumbled. "Would you like to sit down? Uh, just a minute the girls will clear a seat for you."

At this he waved his hand at the two shabbily dressed teens in the corner. Doris would later compare the whole experience as one which out-did anything Dickens wrote. Accepting the now available chairs, the two visitors began.

"OK, Mr. Gertz. We're here NOT as gossipy old neighbors with time on their hands but caring neighbors who cannot bear to see such a disaster as you have been through take place without offering a hand up."

"What are you talking about? Everything's alright here. Take a look around." Gus said with a gesture. The girls are doing fine, Andre is ...alive...the house is a bit neglected but..." His tears could not be stopped.

He fell into Ella's arms completely out of control.

"OK, Mr. Gertz. It's alright to weep, even to curse the gods, but at some point you must get on with it. Take a really good look around here. You've got 3 children here who need you. You have a wonderful home that is falling into disarray. What in the world do you think your gentle, kind wife would be thinking now? What would she wish you to do?" said Ella.

"Is this all you can manage? Then at least protect the children from your choice." interjected Doris. "We have a plan that we think could help you but only if you decide to try."

Gus seemed unable to grasp what they were saying. Again, he looked around his home as if seeing it for the first time. But this time he found the energy to look the women in the face.

"You're right, ladies." He gasped. "I have done the worst job at life's disasters of anyone I know. As a matter of fact, I pride myself on the education I have, the books I've read. I have always thought that I could face any adversity and move on. I'm ashamed to admit I have been a colossal failure-a worthless father-a disappointment to my neighbors-a..."

"Oh, for goodness sakes Gus stop this self-pity. Yes, this has been a terrible time in your life but you are young enough and obviously smart enough to know you need to move on. Here, sit down and let us offer out proposition." Ella said gently.

He wiped the cool cloth offered by Ella across his eyes then sat down amidst the voluminous debris of his life.

The plan went with no hitches. By June 1946, Ella and Doris couldn't have been replaced by the best do-gooders in all of New England. They went right to work and set their offer on the table. Their bottom line: Doris would be his mainstay helper and others would chip in when needed.

They were correct in their guesses at the business he had established. Doris told them that it would need to be at least $20 per week. He accepted immediately. As a matter of fact, his face began to brighten as he brought up his business success. His business had flourished as Roosevelt's 'new deal' put people back on their feet during the '40's. With so many people out of work at that time he had been able to bring in many good bargains for a minimal fee but that would change, he said. The big war the country was now in again was opening many a spot for a business. Suddenly he appeared to be anxious to begin.

Doris started the following Monday. She would work weekdays from 8AM until the girls got home and settled around 4PM. Each of the other women would come in for one morning for 4 hours to help with cleaning, the laundry, grocery shopping etc. By 4:30 Doris would leave a snack for them and a prepared supper. Then the girls would take over. The agreement was that Gus would be home by six in the evening, he would have supper with them, and then help with homework before they went to bed. Baby Andre Jan Gertz's life was finally off and running.

The girls did their best adjusting to the new woman in the house. The biggest problem was that they missed their mother so dreadfully. Maude had known all about caring and nurturing. She knew just how to make a bruise feel better or what they needed if they didn't feel well or just wanted to learn how to make pies or... There were a thousand things Maude's sunny personality made better. She had held the family together many times.

Doris was a person of intelligence and compassion. She did not want to take Maude's place. She often asked the girls for advice.

"Millie, what outfits do you like the best? Do you have a favorite sandwich to go in your lunch box? Or, would you rather have lunch in the school cafeteria? Hilda, I'll bet you'd like to have your own bureau, right? I know I can arrange that. And by the way, girls, where are the clothes and other nursery items for Andre kept?"

The girls were soon happy to have a woman in the house. Their personal hygiene improved and with the help of Susan, they soon were enjoying life at BHS very much. The house shone again as well. By spring, Andre Jan was beginning to sit up and eat some of the mashed vegetables Doris offered him; it seemed to Hilda and Mildred as if there was a light at the end of the Gertz' tunnel.

Unfortunately, their father did not recover as well. His melancholy grew deeper and he became more distant with each year it seemed. He did insist that his girls get an education and try to acquire a skill that would help them survive. He saw to it that they spend at least one hour each evening reading one of the many classics he and Maude had brought from Belgium. This was followed by another hour of

36

discussion, then a snack, then bed. The girls did well but as they moved on towards graduation from BHS, he was done with their future. He was sure they would be clever enough to attract a good man and because of Doris' care they knew how to be good wives. They didn't need him for much he realized.

He was attentive to the one thing he knew a lot about: his outside business. By the time Andre was five years old all attention was on getting him educated and ready for school. He entered first grade in the fall of 1951 and devoured the books and any information he could glean from his teachers.

From the age of eight, Gus kept Andre at his side insisting that he learn the business. By the time Andre was 18 he had graduated BHS and was thinking about a possible college scholarship.

The small business had thrived. Unfortunately, their 10 acres soon filled with the town's throw-a-ways and the town meetings got more and more strident about what they considered an eyesore. Gus had never asked for any favors from town folk and had made friends in many places but he soon realized that he would need to change.

By 1960, as Andre entered his junior year at UNH, Gus sold his crumbling yard over to the Rollin's builders. He kept the house and five acres to the northwest in hopes that Andre might use it. He used a good deal of his profits from the sale to buy himself a truck which would make his business more modern. He then went through all of the leftovers he had in the little shop in the barn and bought half a block in the Main Street area.

He decided to open the town's first hardware store on Main Street. The store flourished to the point where he was able to begin remodeling and enlarging his hardware store, and then he looked for other pastures. The block he had kept behind his store soon became GERTZ EMPORIUM and was loaded with whatever could be had from his barn. He was intent on leaving it all to Andre but never on showing his son real love. There was just none left after Maude.

The neighborhood surrogates who had seen to Andre's needs kept track of him. All were happy to see the fruits of their kindness.

37

They had taught him to be well groomed, to be on the lookout for those who would be jealous or destructive to his goal. From his first year in school they had emphasized that he needed to set goals. In retrospect, the diversity of the women who had guided and cared for him through his teens had given him some useful tools. Each one had a different style and loved to communicate it to this protégé of theirs. Andre soon became easy with others. His gift for gab attracted all with whom he became acquainted. By the time he finished BHS he had become a trusted leader as well as Valedictorian. He was a handsome young man and more educated than half of the townsmen. Soon he took his many 'mothers' advice and established a goal. It would be to be a major player in Branfield's politics.

He surmised that it would be to his advantage to accept the scholarship he had received from UNH and study social studies and government. He was going to be in charge of whatever Branfield would need and then...who knew? Maybe even the state. In '67, with four years of college under his belt, Andre Jan Gertz proudly took his father's place as manager of the hardware store. He deemed it correctly to be one of the best ways to meet and greet the town's movers and shakers and he was right.

The people felt that their town was on the rise. The Rollins' developments had been a huge success and more and more small stores were opening. In addition to Gertz Hardware they now had two drug stores, three garages including a Gulf on the main drag and a TEXACO down by the river, as well as a Five and Dime and a RED and WHITE Grocery on Elm.

Along the way, as Andre moved toward his goal, Gustav had acquired quite a questionable reputation. They were glad the family hardware store was succeeding but they still had a problem with Gustave's second hand emporium in the block behind it.

Every year at the annual town meeting the citizens of Branfield steeled themselves for the inevitable melee that ensued. The noises coming from the auditorium always created a stir. Word was that many people passing by had even dialed 911 in fear for their lives.

The operators had established a routine answer: "Yes, we know about the war on Ash Street. No, there is no danger to you or your family. The dust will settle in a very short time. We are working on improving living conditions for everyone in the town of Branfield and this will soon stop. Thank you for your call."

The question before them was: Was it proper to tolerate the piles of miscellaneous odds and ends that had still accumulated inside and behind GERTZ EMPORIUM? Did the people in the town need to tolerate the crumbling fences around the back of his business? All agreed that Gustav was a good citizen. Most, however, thought the area the town had fenced in behind the stores on Main Street had been intended to supply parking for their Main Street businesses. In fact, they felt, their beautiful town was becoming a garbage dump. Because of the constant influx of new residents more and more people sued, questioned, and made fun of the items brought up.

They admired Andre, but when the subject of the town meeting was his father's backyard business, they came with prepared legal presentations and loud objections to his pleas for his father. Family doesn't give one the right to break the town's rules, they said.

Andre Jan always smiled when he took the podium at the town meetings and then launched into tales of his father's life. He told of the sadness of his mother's loss and the courage it had taken for his father to work and raise a family. He said he wasn't sure most men would have done the same. He mentioned the care he had received in his life from many of the women he could see in the hall and how grateful he and his 'dad' were. At this, many husbands could be seen offering a handkerchief to their wives.

The younger Gertz then addressed the article in question: Should "Old Pap" be allowed to keep his GERTZ EMPORIUM in their town? Much negotiating went on and by the end of the annual March meeting, all who escaped having his or her name bandied about, breathed a sigh of relief when, with a final pounding of the gavel, GERTZ EMPORIUM remained in business. Andre had bought one more year for his father.

During Andre's speech, he had chosen not to mention that he had grown up without any real attention from his now totally depressed father, and had learned how to get almost anything he wanted from his surrogates. That had been almost too easy. They wanted him to like them and he was up to the task of letting them care for him until he could do it himself. Anytime he could, he chose what would be best for Andre. He learned to smile and say thank you while 'picking the brains' of all he met. Andre had goals; goals that only he knew. He had finished college in record time, was now an important leader in Branfield, and was soon being considered as the new town's manager a position that would certainly put him in direct line for their next mayor. It took no time for him to become head of the ELKS, the LIONS, and the BETTER BUSINESS BUREAU, all of whom ran the town.

Along the way he had made copious notes as to what others in town might do for him. He knew most of the foibles of the town fathers and if truth be told, many of the town mothers and sisters as well. Before the first gavel had sounded in any new town meeting, many cups of coffee and handshakes at HERM'S Bar and BETTY'S took place. Even though he would have wished for a pat on the back or even a handshake, his handling of the situation reinforced his belief that he could do almost anything.

Gus passed away in his sleep on an April Sunday in 1979, announcing that he was happy to be joining his life's love once more. His two daughters had married and moved to a small town in Maine. They arrived for the funeral and then announced to Andre that they had no desire to live in Branfield. It was growing too fast. They wanted the bucolic living style that only Maine could offer. He was free to take over whatever their father had left. Andre thanked them. Then, now in his prime at 47 years old, wished them well, collected the monies his father had and remodeled the hardware store. He then auctioned off a lot of the Emporium's stock, and had the block cleared to be used as parking for the town's shoppers. He was now top dog in Branfield. Without looking back, he set himself to considering what would be the next move for him.

He reviewed his success and made a momentous decision. Something was missing. He was a man of purpose, of wealth, of intelligence. He demanded and got respect at all times. He had recognition in the town-he might run for state office he thought. He spent hours ruminating on his life and his future. Within a week he had his newest goal: he would go into the politics of the town, probably run for mayor and then the hit the state capitol in Concord. What he needed was a wife.

For weeks he gave this a great deal of thought. He knew nearly everyone in the town. There had always been a matron or two being obvious about introducing him to their daughters. In fact, in the modern times of the '70's the daughters themselves had often made a play but he'd been too busy to indulge for longer than a couple of evenings out. He made lists of what he would expect from a wife. The word love never landed on his list. He wasn't sure he wanted children but decided it would be just fine to have a son who he could train to do and be whatever he, Andre, wanted of him. He kept watch over new town arrivals. No one fit his bill.

Suddenly it struck him. Of course, this would work. She would be exactly what he needed: an honest, loyal person in a position of power in town, a person who had never been married, and most of all, a woman who would be grateful for his advances. He made a plan immediately.

The first thing he needed was to know a great deal more about her. He knew just who would help and immediately called his favorite care taker, Nancy Hall, and made an appointment to talk. She was aging now but had always been the one of the five he could manipulate. She would be the one who would keep his privacy as well he was sure. His guess was correct on his choice. Nancy was ecstatic to receive the call and they set a date for the next day. She was a font of information and by the time they had eaten two of her apple fritters and drank coffee for a couple of hours, he had the life of Gladys Morgan Medford well in hand-not only in hand but recorded for him to review later.

41

GLADYS MORGAN MEDFORD

June 9, 1962, was a Friday night again. Gladys Morgan Medford sat alone in the Branfield High gym. The basketball game was tied. The crowd was going wild. The cheerleaders had a routine right before their best cheer-the one where Julie climbed to the top of their pyramid.

"Are you ready?" they shouted. The audience roared: "YES. YES. YES." And Julie began her climb. The cheer rang through the rafters.

"Yay Rob. Yay McCain

Help us all to

Win this game."

The crowd acknowledged approval with great cheers and stomping of their feet on the worn grandstand floors. The second big cheer came as Julie completed her summersault down to her place in line, the whole place exploded:

"GO BADGERS. GO BADGERS. GIVE IT TO 'EM, BOB."

What they needed was three points and with the next pass from Harvey, their star forward, Bob McCain scored a three. The BHS basketball team was state champ again. Bob became the school's hero for the last time as this was the final game for seniors. All was happiness and light in their town but not so much for Gladys. Ugly reality struck her like an ax. She was alone and lonely. She looked around and found no one who gave a darn about her and if truth be told she supposed, no one except Bob McCain who she longed to impress. With further perusal of the evening, Gladys realized that was how it was going to be until June graduation. Even though Gladys and Julie had been friends for the whole four years this looked like a chasm that could not be mended. The bold facts: the Badgers were on a roll, the town's citizens were proud to be #1 in the state, and Bob was ogling Julie. She'd been defeated.

After the June festivities, Gladys wished her few friends good luck, and made plans to go to the small accounting school just over the Massachusetts' line. It would take 2 years and she had gotten her parents to agree that she could stay in a dorm for the duration or her classes. She felt she needed to regroup, to build some kind of life away from Branfield. There were no scales that would have measured her excitement at living her own life even if it was only fifty miles away. It was so good to get away from her caring but aged parents and their old fashioned ways.

It was never her intention to settle back in the area, even. In fact once she had had her own dorm room and been at the tech college for a couple of years she longed to see even more of the world-maybe even New York or, in her really wildest dreams, maybe Los Angeles! Who knew? She told herself. With the early May phone call on her graduation day, an accounting degree firmly in her possession, the dream was shattered.

Her mother telephoned to inform her that she wouldn't be able to come to the graduation because there had been a tragedy. Her father had been visiting across the street when he'd suddenly collapsed. The neighbor had called 911 but it had been to no avail. Dad had passed away.

Gladys' plans flew out the window in an instant. The truth of the situation stayed with her in spite of her efforts to obliterate it. Her parents were much older than most. She was a late and only child born in her mother's 44th year. Her mother had not been in great health since the late birth and there would be no one else who could help her. Gladys needed to go home.

It took three months before she got her mother better organized and felt it would be alright to leave her at home each day. She had taken time to look over her mother's finances. The family had never had much income but they had managed to finish paying for the little home on Birch Street in the first Rollins development, and her father had situated them so that her mother could live on Social Security. Barely, but survive. For the foreseeable future they could get by but Gladys knew

43

she needed to do more, not only for the money but also for her own sanity. She needed to get out and exist, even if it had to be in Branfield. A month later, at the age of 22, Gladys Medford was back in the small town she no longer wanted to call home, looking for work.

In November of 1964, On a Monday morning Branfield's town manager, Mr. Blandish, looked up as the office door opened, hoping to see just the woman or young lady who would fit the bill as his secretary. He had been less than impressed by the second person who arrived to interview an hour before. She had been flashily dressed, her blouse revealed more than his wife would ever approve of and to top it all off she wore a pair of spike heels. Might be nice to look at, but he knew he'd better not. His musings were interrupted by second light knock on the open door.

"Come in." he said glancing at the paperwork on his desk. "Good Morning. You must be Gladys Medford. Yes? Come in. please." He said as he stood.

"Yes sir." Gladys said as she approached and stood in front of his desk.

The person who stepped into the room was absolutely not like the last one. Gladys was tall, rather plump and very plain. She wore no make-up as far as he could see, she was soft spoken, and he would say business-like. The tweed suit looked a bit old fashioned but who was he to know? He thought his wife, Rita, would say her hair was 'dirty blond', neither blond nor brown and her glasses far too big for her face. Certainly the black rims didn't complement her in any way. Still, he liked the proud way she stood, quietly waiting for him to move on. There was no sign of nervousness. He had the immediate impression that she could handle any crisis with aplomb.

"Oh, yes. Please take a seat." He said from his reverie. "I have looked over your application and it is very impressive. I have just a few more questions as it was very thorough."

One hour later Gladys Morgan Medford had a new job. Happiness and depression set in at the same time. My God! She was back in Branfield. Maybe she would be able to manage while her mother needed her and then use this experience to garner a better position elsewhere. A smile came over her face as she remembered what Julie would say to this attitude.

"There you go again, Gladys, polishing up your Mary Janes whenever it poured on your parade. I wonder what will get you to just get mad and jump up and down and wish it were different."

Gladys smiled at the remembrance but couldn't seem to think how to do all that. She headed home. It was 5-o-clock; time for her mother's supper.

The job seemed to fit the bill. She got along fine with the employees at City Hall. She asked no questions and neither did they. If they did, her short answers brought a halt to any office gossip. Lisa Grimes who worked at the tax collector's office, asked her a couple of times if she'd like to join the crew on Friday after work. They regularly drove over to Howard's for a cool down after the week but she had refused saying she needed to get home to her mother. After a while they just wished her a nice weekend and let it go at that. Gladys soon became a constantly working shadow who disappeared at five on the dot.

One day in May of 1967, Mr. Blandish (she always called him that even though he said it would be OK if she used Carl) called her into his office with a request.

"Gladys I want you to know what a great job you have been doing as my receptionist. At the same time we will soon have a vacancy in the Tax department and I'm wondering if you would like to be in charge of our tax collector's office. It would be more work maybe but it would also pay more. I think it would be good for us to have a trained accountant leading that department and also I'm considering having it lead to you taking over as Branfield's Town Clerk. Is this anything you'd like to try?"

She was dumbfounded. She'd been at City Hall for three years. Her mother was now 91 and failing. Her life seemed so entrenched in day to day responsibilities. Could she handle more obligations?

45

"I...well..." she started and then caught herself. Maybe this was a good thing. Maybe she could find someone to stay with her mother during the day. Surely they could use the money.

"Mr. Blandish, I can't thank you enough for this opportunity. Could I have this weekend to mull it over? It isn't that I don't want to move up it's just that I do have some things at home that might need reorganizing.

"Oh. Of course, Gladys, take a week if you need. These changes won't be made until the first of April anyway. I tell you what. Let's leave it that the offer is on the table for a couple of weeks. You get back to me as soon as possible, please."

"Thank you so much for the offer. I am glad that you felt I deserved this chance. I will think this over and let you know right away. Have a nice weekend."

With that she left for home. The cod and mashed potatoes were cooked and eaten by 6, a dish of ice cream doled out for dessert and once her mother was settled in front of Jeopardy, she had time to think.

Now what? She asked herself. If I take this job I'm much more committed than I want. Mom would do very well in the assisted living home she had found and she...let 'see...If I sell the house I'll be fine. I would be able to go on a trip...maybe even see Europe. The ifs and buts haunted her sleep for the weekend. Then she suddenly accepted reality. Face it, Gladys, she thought. You are not in a great financial position. Why not take the job. Save for a while longer and then take those trips you so want? Be practical. Set yourself up here in Branfield. Put off your dreams for a little while.

In May 1967, she went directly to the town manager's office and became Branfield's first female tax collector.

The office personnel were not surprised by Mr. Carl Blandish's choice. No one could produce a reason to doubt Gladys' honesty, loyalty, or trustworthiness. Boring, perhaps, but just right for this job and as it happened the job of Town Clerk that she took on six years later.

Quietly, Gladys took over the organizing of the town offices. More and more businesses and political organizations even began to ask her for her opinions. Her salary was voted on by the town council and each year they saw to it that she received the most they could allow. She was able to salt away nearly half of her salary each week. How could she change anything? Her mother's savings and Social Security were enough to live in an assisted care facility. She had grown senile in her waning years and she was in a memory area that prohibited her release. Gladys felt she didn't even recognize her own daughter anymore. Coupled with the sadness this left her with a chance to finally filling some of her own dreams.

By 1980 one would have thought Gladys would be on top of the world. She should have been happy, settled, looking forward to a life of plenty. She was depressed, lonely, and despondent.

A million times a week she asked herself, "Is this all life is about? Here I am 38 years old. Stuck in the one place I swore I would not be, Branfield. I haven't even seen New York let alone Paris."

The realization was hard to accept. Still, she made no effort to engineer a change. Little did she know her life would be entirely different with the sudden arrival at her desk of Andre Jan Gertz.

GLADYS AND ANDRE

The word was that she'd never had an affair; that she kept pretty close to her mother; that she was a wonderful business woman but very shy. Would she appreciate romance or should he keep his approach quiet and gentle. He made his decision and was to put it in place.

"This is it." Andre said to himself. "Make it good today or all else could be lost."

Oh no. She thought. I must get out of here on time. My mother needs me and I've got the other responsibility. I'm going to have to make decisions soon. What could he want? It's probably some kind of research he wants me to do. I really want to finish the afghan I've started. I must steal myself and refuse.

47

"Hello, Mr. Gertz. I hope you are well. If you'll excuse me I must be off on time." She said firmly as she started around her desk to leave.

"Ah, just a minute of your time please?" Andre offered. "Would it be alright if I called you Gladys? I was wondering if you would be interested in having a cup of coffee with me. Or, maybe tea?" He said as he saw her blanch. "I've wanted to ask for a long time but..." As if out of words he turned to go.

"What?" Gladys uttered. "You would like me to have coffee? Why? Where? When? Right now?" She couldn't stop herself. You're blithering, for goodness sakes, she muttered. Get a hold of this. Look up. Is he still there?

"Uh, certainly Mr. Gertz, but I don't have a lot of time. I need to be home soon."

"That will be fine." said Andre as he extended his arm. Gladys grabbed it in need of support. Were there people looking as they left the town hall? What was she to say? It had been so long since she was alone with a man or anyone else for that matter; idle chatter was not at her command. As it turned out, her worries were unfounded. Andre kept up a patter and all she needed to do was listen. Well!

"Gladys, could I encourage you to call me Andre?" he said quietly. "I'm hoping we might get to know each other better soon."

They entered Betty's Coffee Shop just around the corner and were directed to seat themselves. Before she knew it he was escorting her to her chair and had pulled it out for her. Seating himself on the opposite side, he began:

"So, what would you like? Do you drink your coffee with special cream? Maybe Decaf? Would you like a tea cake to go with it?"

The few patrons in the small café hung on every word. Had anyone else ever seen Gladys Medford with a woman friend never mind a man? In fact, had anyone ever seen her with anyone at all?

"It almost looks like a date!" said Jane Collins.

"Call the local gossip sheet, I say." Her friend Lorraine whispered.

48

For the next few months the most talked about couple in Branfield could be found on Thursdays at BETTY'S as soon as the 5 o'clock hour struck.

The town was fascinated but no one was able to think of a reason for or against it. As far as the citizens knew it had been an odd but happy decision. The couple kept very much to themselves. Soon, Andre hired Jack Lemire, Harry Sykes, and Adam Rollins, all builders from Rollins Inc., to run his store.

Gladys continued to keep the town's business running smoothly, while he quietly lined up support for his run for Mayor. Chief Jim watched the whole dance and wondered if that was a good thing for Gladys but every time he saw her heading for work as he cruised by, she looked more and more confident; in charge of herself, ready to be happy.

For the next few months the most talked about couple in Branfield could be found on Thursdays, at BETTY'S as soon as the 5 o'clock hour struck. Helen, from the town hall workforce even said that she had heard they were planning on getting married-word spread far and wide.

One day in June, the couple announced by a small ad in the local society page of the BRANFIELD RECORD, that they were engaged and would marry in December. Andre's sisters came to visit their brother in July to gain information on the big event and found time to gossip a bit with Gladys' old friend Julie. Julie made the assumption that her friend was happy and couldn't resist putting the details out. Soon, everyone knew that the two newlyweds would be living in Branfield in Andre's father's house, that Andre was building a new home he called GERTZ MANOR, and that they had made a pact not to have children. There wasn't much else to know.

The couple kept very much to themselves, she basking in his attention, and he, working toward his success. Knowing he would need free time to set up his ultimate goal, Andre encouraged Gladys to continue keeping the town's business running smoothly, reporting to him each day about how the town was run.

49

The shocker came on a Thursday in August. The two were chatting quietly at Betty's when Gladys had obviously announced something momentous. No one heard the details but patrons said Andre Jan's countenance turn into rage. They added that Gladys blanched and pulled her hand away, almost in fear. Suddenly he pulled her up from the chair and the two sped from the café.

"Wow!" announced Marge. "That's something new. Looks like a big crisis it you ask me."

"Probably asked mousy Gladys for a little action before the wedding." offered Fred. "I don't know if she's up to it."

"Please, Fred. Must there be something sexy to everything you do? Can't a couple ever have an argument without it mentioned? Come on. Let's get home and watch CNN."

"Yeah well, I'll bet..."Fred went on as Marge dragged him up the sidewalk.

For the next few months the couple's brouhaha became topic #1. No one could fill in the blanks but it wasn't for not trying. A fly on the wall would have been astonished at the subject that had caused the ruckus.

"What do you mean you've got an obligation you need to discuss?? Now? We've just agreed to marry in a few months and you surprise me with some problem? We've even published the date? You've got to be kidding. I don't have time for this. You know I have plans for myself." He spoke loudly and then caught himself.

"Uh, I'm sorry, Gladys. I just want to get married and settle down. I wanted us to be happy and I know we can be successful. So, alright, tell me, what's this big thing? Does it require some involvement on my part? I don't have much free time, you know. Can it be fixed? Will it spoil my place in Branfield?" Andre nearly screamed when they were seated in the car.

Gladys should have noticed that there was no mention of her happiness or of their future. Her chosen had a one track mind she realized and almost decided to call everything off but her loneliness and sense of honor won over and she kept quiet.

"It really is a big thing I know." She stated "And I promise I will handle all of the work that will need to be done. The thing is, my Aunt Harriet over in Connecticut, has been caring for her daughter's son for five years. Edith never did get married and then she got involved in drugs and ...well you can imagine. Harriet felt responsible at that time and took the boy in. He was five years old. Now, five years later I've just been notified that Harriet needs to go into a nursing facility. There are no other relatives to step in now that she has reached her 85th year. In fact, as far as I know, there are no other Medfords even. Rather than have the boy placed in an orphanage, I promised some time ago that I would raise him if this should happen."

"Raise a child who's not my own???' Andre whispered through gnashed teeth. "No way! I've even hoped we might be able to have one. I might like to have a son of my own, you know." Sweat began to collect on his forehead. "You can't be serious, Gladys. This doesn't fit my plan at all. I want you to find a good place for him and let's get on with our lives."

"I don't know how I can back out now." Gladys said quietly. "I would be devastated if this breaks us up but if I have to I have decided that I would bring him to Branfield and raise him as my own. Should we discuss it further?"

"Discuss it further? My God, Gladys, we have it made just as it is. I've positioned myself to be important in this town-maybe even the state, and you're so important that you'll be the best helper ever. I believe we can own this town with effort and planning. What we don't need is an orphan kid to take care of-especially one with unknown genes. Didn't you say he was black? Look. He has blond hair!" He sneered as he looked at the photo she had produced. He wiped the water from his forehead and added, "I say you give it two more days and see if you really want to sacrifice all that we have going." With that, he slammed his foot on the gas and took her back to her house.

She was totally surprised not only at the vitriol she saw from his reply, but also at the backbone she was showing. Perhaps there was no way they could settle this, Gladys thought as she reviewed his blow-up.

51

The last few weeks had been an eye opener. She'd talked herself into changing her mind about "waiting 'til the wedding night" and never regretted it. Each night he arrived at her home was sheer excitement for her. What a change from the reasons she had had for years when she needed to be home at 5. He was so experienced and such a gentle teacher. How much would she miss that feeling she got when he touched her, kissed her. Could she do without the closeness that gave her such happiness? What had she known about love? She'd never even given it a thought since her teen age years. Now, she quivered at every touch of his hand.

How much she had loved the last few weeks of anticipation. The way her body reacted when he climbed into her bed and began caressing her skin. The thrill of gay abandon that washed over her always left her breathless. She was amazed that he was hers. If she took Paul in, maybe she would have to go back to being the old maid in town. There was no way she could imagine doing that. She questioned everything she had become, finally saying to herself: you've had disappointments before. Wait. Think. This will all work out soon.

"What is the matter with me? I wonder if I could talk to Julie. We were good friends once and maybe that was what I need." She muttered out loud one day. She called Julie.

JULIE AND GLADYS

Julie agreed to meet almost before she asked. She added that she was on her second marriage and Saturday was the only day she could leave her two kids. That fit perfectly with Gladys' work. By Saturday on a bright blue afternoon the two sat in a corner of the new park that Andre had donated. The sun shone through the maples trying to brighten Gladys' mood without much luck. And she felt really unsettled when she saw her old friend come strolling toward her.

Gladys was taken aback. Julie didn't look a day older than she did in high school. She was slim and her black hair shone brightly in the pony tail she wore. She was dressed in faded jeans and a pretty pea green tee that set the whole thing off.

"I'm so glad you could come." Gladys said with a hug. "You look wonderful, you know. Are you sure you weren't just a baby when I knew you at BHS? And by the way I was so sorry to hear of your break-up with the great basketball man. What happened?"

"I don't know. I guess I didn't realize I couldn't always be the cheer leader and wanted him to take a turn. All he thought of was sports and getting hired on some big team. Money became an issue you can guess. Then we had two kids...well I had two kids...he never took responsibility for them. It goes on and on. There were some good and some bad times but Joe Gilburn is just what I need. Oh, sorry. I'm really running on aren't I? And you look great. What's happened in your life to make such a difference? Is there love in the air? Are the rumors I've heard true? And, with our leading politician? What a catch!" Julie prattled on.

"That's what I was hoping you could help me with." opened Gladys. "You've never made fun of my shyness and I'm in a real dilemma right now. Plus, I really like my job and now there's a big hitch. Yes. I've been seeing Andre Gertz. It was his idea, I have no clue why. But there he was one day, standing at my desk asking me out and..." She paused trying hard to continue.

"Now, something has come up that could ruin everything. I'm probably going to lose him with my stubbornness but I have no choice I don't think. I can't believe I could love someone like him." She stared directly into her friend's eyes; her voice wavered as she spoke. "At least I had him for a while. So, is this, what love is?" She said sadly. "I had no idea it could be so wonderful. I feel so young almost. I... giddy, I guess; and now this. There's got to be a compromise somewhere." She rose and walked around the hedges desperately looking for control.

"OK, Julie." She said into the air. "Does it always have to be me who fixes things? Do I have to give up the best thing that ever happened to me? Is there something I'm missing here?"

"Well, Gladys. This sounds serious. There's a food truck over near Main St. Let's get ourselves something to munch on and settle down for the afternoon. I think you need to tell me from the beginning. I've already told Joe I'd be late so, what the heck is going on?"

By 4-o-clock in the afternoon, between hotdogs and fries, Gladys had done a fairly thorough job of explaining her problem.

She ended her tale with: "So, you see, I don't feel I can let my aunt down never mind this poor boy. He's only ten years old as I said and there's no one else. But God! I can't imagine giving up on Andre. We've had such a good time together. I had no idea what it would be like to anticipate a lover coming home at night or asking me for help with his problems, or just working together planning a new house. It has been the highlight of my life. Now..." her voice trailed off as she gripped her hands together to stop the tremors that had started.

"Well. You've gotten yourself in a real pickle, I'd say." Julie started. "I guess the first thing I see that stands out is a question I'd ask myself. Am I the only one in this relationship? Doesn't it take two to tango? I've had a man who only thought of himself and his goals. His insistence on my unwavering support for him at all times shot our relationship down. I'm not saying this guy of yours is like that, Gladys, but I think you need to really spend some hours analyzing what it is you want your life to look like in a few years. You need to face it. This red hot thing you two have going is going to wane and you're going to want to just live. Sorry. Have I said too much?" She added.

"No, not at all, my friend, I knew that you'd be honest and helpful. That's why I asked you. Thanks. You've given me a great deal to think about. Listen, I've got to get going. Andre will be home soon. I'll give a lot of thought to your input. Let's try to make ourselves meet more often, OK?"

With that the two friends hugged and went on to their own day.

ANDRE GLADYS AND PAUL

She and Andre didn't speak that night or the next. He still arrived at 5 each afternoon but only ate and then left by nine. The house seemed to be bursting with quiet. She was terrified this might become the norm. Then, two days later as she was getting ready to leave for work, she found Andre pacing the kitchen floor waiting for her. He had obviously used the key she had given him weeks ago but she had not heard him. She had decided the night before that as far as she was concerned the die was cast: she needed his love but the boy needed a home more. She hoped with all her heart that his solution might meet hers at least half way.

As for him, he had made a momentous decision. It was clear, he thought as he drummed his fingers on the counter. He needed her inside knowledge to help him move up the political ladder. She needed the pleasure of raising a child. He formed his plan and waited impatiently for her to settle down.

"Hello, my dear." He offered as she went to fill her coffee cup. "I have decided what I'd like to do. Sorry it took so long but your bomb really shook me. Would it be possible for us to sit down and think about this like adults? I would like to do so now as I think we need to discuss this privately, before you go to work." He was much gentler than the last day she had seen him.

"Of course. What would you like? I could cook up some bacon and eggs. I'd think that would be good. I have some ideas that might work. Just let me make a call to the town hall."

A half hour later the two of them faced each other in Gladys' small den-a fresh cup of coffee in hand. Both were anxious beyond words.

'Why don't you go first, Andre? Then I'll put in my two cents and we'll see what we have." Gladys used her business voice.

"OK. Here goes. I want to say up front. I really don't want to become a parent to a 10 year old mixed-race child. I feel that by then much of his behavior and education will have been formed; especially having been raised on the wild streets of Hartford. I have very strong feelings about education and training of any youngster, specifically a wild boy. So, I will be willing to let you go ahead with this craziness but I will be the one, and the final one, who will make decisions about his upbringing for the foreseeable future."

His words fell before her like lead. What did he mean? 'His orders?' 'His discipline?' Where did he get these views? Where did she fit in? Was she a wife, a partner, or some kind of foundation for him to use in some kind of political quest?

"I have written a list of things that I would need to have you agree to before I'd say yes to bringing the boy into our lives. I hope you'll see their validity and approve them. Then I think we should get on with our lives and other decisions for ourselves." He added.

My God, Gladys told herself as she read his list. Paul would be raised in Andre's image. He was to be the only one to educate the boy. He thought that might take 3-4 years. No one else was to be informed of the fact that they had taken in a 12 year old boy. The child would be kept away from all except the two of them during that time. Gladys would be responsible for his food and clothing as well as giving him some companionship, but that was to be all. He had already begun thinking about an adjustment to his homestead and would show it to her that evening. There was to be no discussion about this; no compromise.

Who did I think he was? Her inner voice screamed. She answered her own question. He was handsome, gentle, intelligent, and attentive. Still the pros and cons kept on. It was so good not to be alone. She had never had a boyfriend, let alone one that was interested in her, her job, her knowledge, her. The physical life she now had was more than she could ever have expected. She felt loved; cherished. Was it so? Was that even enough? Yes, it was so good not to feel unloved. But wait a minute. He hadn't even said the magic words in his proposition. When would 'I love you' be first? Should expect that? The bottom line: What would she sacrifice for it? Was this even a fair choice to make her chose? No, of course not. Julie's words echoed in her ears. 'I married a selfish man once...'

"Wait a minute, Andre." She nearly shouted. "This is not about the boy is it? It seems to me you just want a servant or are taking advantage of my knowledge of the town. Do you care for me at all? What a fool I've been!" She rose and stomped over to the window, trying to catch her breath.

"No. No. My dear, please calm down." Andre rose and took her hands in his as he spoke. "I didn't mean to come off as a control freak. I guess I was just blown away at the blockade that was being put in front of what I hoped for our future. I feel like I'm just learning how I might be a good husband and here I am being asked to be a father. For that matter, do you know anything about being a mother?" He paused, letting that settle.

"Oh, for goodness sakes!" Gladys said in an impatient tone. "We both had mothers; imperfect sometimes, maybe. I did anyway, and she was supportive. I could have wished she had taught me more about the real world but that's how it goes. She was a simple woman. She never asked for much except my immediate presence when she was in trouble. Unfortunately for me, I guess, I was born just as you were when it was past time for her to handle a child. I loved her and I didn't have any idea about other kinds of love. How about you? "

"Well, I didn't have a real mother you know. Mine died when I was born. But I did have Doris every day. She was always supportive. She was happy, helpful and full of life. The rest of the women were very good to me."

"Still, ii wasn't easy for me. I suffered more than you know. My father never was able to help me. He was so involved in his own depression, and as a matter of fact, I believe he died wishing she had lived and I had not. I think he wanted to die every day. He just let anything happen to us kids. Lucky for the girls they were 11 and 12 when our mother died but me? I was a baby. Before I was 1 year old I was being taken care of by a do-gooding neighbor. Yes. She was kind. She kept the girls in school and safe. But her time was limited.

"My sisters were another ball of wax. They were in charge of me every day from 4 -6 and let me tell you it was not a good thing. I remember being totally neglected most of the time. They wanted nothing to do with me. They'd come home and close the door to my room. Then, they'd raid the fridge and take all they could find to munch while watching TV. I'm guessing, but I think they ran around and picked up about fifteen minute before dad got home. He was always pleased at what they had done and then more of less ignored the three of us throughout supper. I think I cried every day until I was five. Then dad gladly sent me off to elementary school. There was no doubt in my mind that he had no idea how to care for us.

"Good old Doris kept our home fires burning at least. She was kind but not too bright, you know. She loved training Millie and Hilda to cook and clean. By the time I was ten they were ready for the kind of boring marriage she had and I was in nowhere land.

"All through high school, good old dad began to train me to help him run his business. I learned to drive the truck to collect the things that kept his mind busy. You know, as I think about it I guess that's what kept him alive as long as it did.

"He did value education as you know so he insisted that I go to college right after BHS. I had the highest GPA of all of the senior class but I don't think he even cared. Anyway, I got a scholarship to UNH and lucky for Branfield and its citizens, I fell into history, social studies and political science. Along the way I realized that I was quite interested in politics and that I needed to know more about business so I loaded my schedule up with courses stressing business and politics in my final year.

"Old Gus never did come to my graduation. By then he was only into his repair and antique business when he could find time while nursing his depression. He never got over the fact that his Maude had died. I wonder if he ever really loved any of us kids. He never told us so." His voice trailed off and he seemed to drift away.

"In '67, I came home with my big degree and took over running the hardware store. Before I realized it, I had parlayed it into a successful business and was bored. I wanted more. I found it right in front of my eyes. I began to attend all of the town's meetings and voting became an obsession. I'd never been social but it became obvious that I needed to join the high mucky-mucks if I wanted to be a politician.

Soon, as you know, I will be voted in as the town's mayor. I'm going places, Gladys. Will you help and come with me?"

Gladys' heart melted at this private information. He needed love. She wanted someone to love and knew she would never do better. Still, was he really in need of unconditional love or abeyance? Was she the one to give it to him? What did he plan on giving in return? When she had agreed to marry him she had done so for selfish reasons. She was lonely. She was flattered by his attention. There would be a nice home and maybe in time he would give her a chance to raise Paul Middleton as her own son, a person to love and care for. Intelligence took a back seat. The pull was too great. Maybe she should compromise about the boy. Perhaps she could manage the marriage without giving up too much. She didn't dare look the list over again.

"Andre, my dear, what is it you want? How can I help and where does the boy fit in? I love you, you know. I think we can be very happy and would like to adopt the child. By the way, his name is Paul Richard Middleton. I think we should get used to calling him Paul. I will make arrangements to have him here right after we marry on December 10. "

THE END OF OUR RESEARCH

Marion made three copies of what she'd done and then sent out an immediate text to her two friends. The text read:

Hi ladies. Wow! You two certainly covered the bases in a hurry. I'm sure we have more than enough to set our curiosity off. I have taken the time to organize your notes and will send you copies soon. I think it would be just fine to meet here next Wednesday, instead of waiting 2 weeks. Miss you both already. Let me know and I'll fix and do for lunch.

The next morning she sent the copies and by afternoon she received notes from both of them. They were fascinated at her speedy work and yes, they would be at her home the following Wednesday, May 25.

CHAPTER IV

CALAMITY

The house was clean, the kids had called, and the day lay barrenly before her. Marion poured herself another cup of coffee and thought about how bored she was. Then it struck her. What was the matter with her mind? For goodness sakes, it was "WALLOWING WEDNESDAY"- the name thanks to Octavia. It was time for the tête-à-tête. Where in the world did Monday and Tuesday go? Well, OK. Better get changed and on the move. This is always fun and sometimes even exciting.

Marion looked so forward to this little bit of socialization. Now that she retired and with the pandemic's arrival, it was a special way to feel alive. Of course today's meet would have to be more subdued. That little jaunt for shopping and ice cream last week had lifted their spirits no end, but this week needed to be different. According to all of the news media, good old Covid-19 had reared its ugly charms again had turned up with something called Omicron. She was not up to taking a chance on the outside world. In fact she had made an appointment for the booster shot the CDC was recommending. I bet the other two haven't even thought of it. She supposed that would be topic #1.

They were to meet at Octavia's this week. There she was sure the three of them would come up with something even more world-shattering to rant about. Octavia had been in a crazy mood for a while now; maybe she was back with Jim. Who knew what that had been about? Perhaps we'll get her to spill the details. Better still, we must rehash whether last week's research had made a difference in anyone's understanding of their town's mayoral/senator situation. Topic #2.

Hope they like this new yellow sweater I ordered. Lord knows they'll tell me. Not complaining she told herself. Let's face it, with the exception of Hal; this friendship had been the best thing that had happened to her probably in a lifetime. She wondered if either of them felt the same. Alright, that'll be topic #3, she thought.

For some reason Martha had called and asked for a lift. Not like her at all; Marth was by far the most independent one of them. Marion couldn't remember any other time she had requested a favor. Hmmm. Topic #4?

Finally, there would be Topic #5: the research.

Then she took a final look at her aging self as she passed the hall mirror. Not bad-still in a size 12 jean and fairly slim. She wished she hadn't lost the couple of inches in height though. She'd spent most of her years able to stare into the average man's eyes and now it seemed she was always looking up.

"Ah well. Get on with this day." She sighed to herself. In a minute she found her keys and headed to the garage.

As she drew up to the beautiful Victorian she marveled as always at Martha's sense of style. The slate blue exterior melted into the greens of the blue spruce on either side of the home and the bright spring daffodils along the long brick walkway leading to the barn-red door couldn't be more welcoming she thought. Today the early spring sun lit the whole place up and highlighted the orange-breasted robins that flocked around her yard.

"I really love Hal and my house on the hill. The views are spectacular and those sunrises! Still, this is beautiful." She said as Martha strolled slowly down the walk.

"Well done, my friend. You've made this place a bandbox for anyone to see." She added as Martha opened the side door. "Hi, ho, by the way and a how are you? Well, I hope."

Martha nodded and reached for her seat belt in silence. For the next mile and a half to Octave's condo not a word was spoken.

"What's going on, Marth? Are you not feeling well? I've got some aspirin if you need a couple; or maybe a bit of wine this afternoon?"

Marion could see this was not a good path and just pulled into the recently completed gated condo-complex coming to a stop at number 32. Martha had not moved. Even when Octavia spied them from her balcony and waved, she didn't acknowledge.

What the devil??? Marion thought. Give her space and we'll see.

She tried again. "Isn't this the best day ever? New England can sure rival any other place in the world when she puts her mind to it. I'm happy it's Wednesday. I don't know about you, but boredom had set in at my place. It's so good to be here! Right Marth?" There was no answer.

They had reached the open door swung wide by their friend and still not a word from Martha. Something had to be wrong.

"Greetings friends, come on in. On a day like this I thought we'd hang out on the deck. There are umbrellas and a gorgeous afternoon sun will be with us soon. I've got a nice bottle of wine cooling and a few goodies. Let's head out there." Octavia said between hugs all around. And so they settled for an afternoon of chatter and comradery.

Suddenly there were guttural sounds coming from Martha's corner. A quiet rumble underlined each sentence Marion and Octavia put forth. Both of them turned at once. Martha was holding her body at an angle. She was doubled over, her head in her hands. Her whole being was shaking. A waterfall made its way through her fingers, refusing to be dammed up any longer. Her two friends each took a side, arms extended, bringing her into their cocoon.

"Whatever it is, Marth, go ahead. Hang on to us. We're here and will always be." They said in unison. Octavia rushed to her bathroom and moistened a soft cloth.

"Here now. Let's see if this will help." She offered as she touched her friend's forehead gently. "Don't say a word. Marion, clear that sofa over there and we'll help her to lie down."

"No. No. No." shouted Martha. "I don't want to lie down. I don't want attention. I don't want cool cloths on my forehead." she moaned as she threw the damp cloth to the deck. "I need it to go away. I need it to stop. I..." with that, she fainted in their arms.

"My God." whispered Octavia. "What could this be? Do you suppose it is one of the twins? Or an accident? Or COVID-19?"

"I have no idea, but let's get her over to that couch. Martha, can you hear me?" she said as she shook her friend gently. "Can you move your legs? Are you in any pain? I see you've opened your eyes." Their friend moved her legs and tried to move. With that they helped her to her feet and laid her carefully-pillowed on the sofa.

"Here have a little sip of this water. Steady now...There. That's better." She added. Martha tried to grasp the glass as Octavia steadied her shaking hand.

"I'm so sorry." Martha moaned weakly. "I shouldn't have tried to come today. It was just that I didn't know where else to turn. I can't seem to breathe. I think I have no organs left in my chest...just a cold black hole...I..." and the sobs came again. "This isn't like me. I should be handling this better...I'm a grown woman...I...GOD DAMMIT! SHIT! F-WORD, F-WORD, F-WORD!" she screamed.

Once more she collapsed. But this time, her color was brighter and the situation became more hopeful to her two friends. She was able to lift the glass and take a sip. She looked around the room seeming to orientate to her surroundings. Then with a determined effort she steadied herself, sat up, and began.

"Dennis has contracted COVID-19." She whispered. "He was tested two days ago. He was admitted immediately. He's critical and they're going to decide if he needs the ventilators etcetera today. I have not told the kids yet, but I must. They won't be surprised that they haven't heard. He isn't home often these day; most of the time I don't know what's going on. He's been working at the damn hospital 24/7 for nearly a year. I tried all morning to think of the words and to keep calm while I told them but...Look at me. I'm an out-of-control woman. I can't even put two sentences together..." The sobs came again. Without a sound she laid back, her eyes closed, and fell asleep.

Octavia carefully placed an afghan over her and motioned Marion inside the living room.

"We've got to get ourselves in hand, Marion. Let's see if we can decide what we can or should do to help." She offered.

"Well, first we need to let her rest for a half hour or so and then have a plan when we wake her." said Marion. "I guess I feel we should find out where the sons are and have them over here. It wouldn't do to tell them at their restaurant, I don't think.

"You're right. Let's see. It's only 2pm. The guys are probably opening the restaurant by 4. They've had to curb their hours you know. No more lunch hours. Mark told me the other day that there was a strong possibility they would have to call it quits unless there's a big turn-around. Apparently, both of them are pregnant." Seeing her friend's puzzled expression she added, "Forgive me Octave, that's the way modern women talk, I'm told. Mark and Cathy are expecting a girl in October, while Mike and Elaine will have a little boy a month later. How wonderful for Marth and Dennis. Oh my God. Did you hear what I just said? Darn it. Why does this have to happen to such a good family? Why our friend?"

"The doctors and scientists all say this thing doesn't care who or what you are, you know. Hey, think that's enough philosophizing. Let's go in and have a chat with Martha. If she agrees, we'll help. I know you have Hal to be with so I can do this if that is a problem."

"Ah Octavia, you're always so damn thoughtful. After we talk to Martha I'll make a call to Hal and we'll hang together as long as she needs us."

With that they sat down near their friend and gently shook her into consciousness. They offered their ideas. She agreed with weak nods and the calls were made. Within an hour both men arrived and they left them with their mother. It didn't take long before they were outside and had made their decision.

"We are taking mom home. We'll be able support whatever she wants. We'll be able to talk to the hospital from there and see just how dire Dad's situation is and then make more plans. I'm told that family members are not allowed in the isolation ward so we'll let you know as soon as we do. Thanks for everything you've done. Wish us luck." With that and heavy hugs, Mark and Michael helped their mother to the car and they were gone.

"Let's sit a minute." said Octavia. "You know, we might all have been exposed. Do you think we'll need to quarantine? What about your kids and Hal? Are we all in danger?"

"Damn. What a world we're in. I don't know. Probably I guess. If you and I have been exposed it would be only from Martha. I'm sure she said she had had her second shot last week. She said the boys hadn't seen their dad for days, so..." she pondered the situation.

The silence was overwhelming. They sat and watched as the sun went downward, speechless, unsure what to do.

The convulsions hit both of them at the same time. With one look between them they began to weep. A friend and her family were in huge trouble. Their hearts were broken as well. Wallowing Wednesday was no longer just a clever description for their mood. The doings of Branfield and the Gertz part had sunken way down on their priority list.

"I did want to tell you, Mare, that Jimmy and I have found a great little bar and grille over in Greenford. It's not too far away;

perhaps 30 miles. It's run by a very pretty young woman and has the most wondrous of all views from great big windows. The river that goes through there is right across the street and it's very wide there. Lots of people have beautiful homes built on the other side. Anyway, the place has a front bar and then many small booths where patrons can just sit and talk. It's very romantic. They've just started to serve light meals too. Jimmy sure loves their steak sandwich.

We've been there two times now as Jimmy likes to get away from town gossip. Guess who I saw lurking in the darkest corner? The mystery man! He looked exactly as your little granddaughter said. Black brimmed hat, black hair, very tall. I told Jimmy about what you knew and he said he'd been going to make time to get over and greet this guy. He said the description had been going around the town. I hope it's OK but I also gave him a copy of the research stuff you typed. He was very happy to have it. He felt it would help him decide if he wants to stay as chief. He's been kind of bored and antsy these days, you know."

"Yes, that's fine with me. Maybe Jim will be able to shine more light on just what goes on at the town hall. I plan on discussing it with Hal this evening. OK, Tavia, that's all for me today. Let's do what we can for Marth and meet again next week. See you then."

BEVERLY A. MASSEY

C H A P T E R   V

CHANCE

He had done it. Life was good for CHANCE & THE STRAGGLERS. They'd made the big time. They were loved, they were wealthy, they were happy with each other. All things he thought he had cared about were going great. It seemed the sun was shining on every one of the band members. Why then had he made his decision? Why did he think it would be OK to upset everyone's applecart? He dreaded telling the guys but guessed they might have had an inkling that something was up for quite a time.

Time---That was it. He needed time to sort out what to do with the feelings that haunted him. It had become his life of late and he knew he must cope with it. In fact, he had decided last night after the bash in OHIO that this set in Boston's Gillette Stadium would be his last. It was scheduled for Saturday, the 25th of June 2022 and would be the end of their present tour. If all things came together maybe he'd be ready for a

January TV appearance or something and maybe the band would be good for a couple more years. That would be 2024 he laughed to himself. With the COVID and the world disasters, who knew? He had to get through June, 2022 and get the boys safely away from his troubles and then deal with it. That's what he was going to do.

In addition, he was going to ask, well demand, that they make some changes in the routine of the show. He didn't want it to be just a carbon copy of the other 12 they had just done. He had sketched out a new show and would ask Luther to present it to them right before the rehearsal this afternoon. No. That's not fair. They've got a week to prepare so he'd ask Luther to postpone this thing today and schedule a couple for next week.

They'd been really successful of late but he knew his playing had been weak and he really didn't care enough to fix it. It will be alright, he assured himself. They had made a lot of money in the past 15 years. If any of the other five guys had any sense they would have saved half. Yeah, well, that's what he hoped anyway.

He certainly needed some space. Hell, they all needed some space. It was settled in his mind. He would call a meet for after the show and make the announcement to them on Sunday. He was tempted to ask Luther, his confidante and manager, to handle the press but thought better of that. There could be no cop-outs if he was to get his life together.

With a light tap on the door, Chance's musings came to a halt. A short, heavily muscled man entered and gently called his name.

"Chance, you've got an interview in 30 minutes. I'll be back in 15 and get you in today's get up. Is there anything else I can help with?"

Chance's heart filled. He thought he'd probably weep something he had not done since he'd left Branfield 25 years ago.

"Luther." The strength in his voice surprised him. "I have something I need to let you know. It's pretty important...No. Wait a minute. As a favor to me, could you plan on an hour or so after the interview so that you and I can talk?" Seeing Luther nod, he continued,

"Also, please let the crew know that I'd like them to meet me at the studio in Newbury, by 11am on Sunday, June 26. Also, I've changed a few things in the way I think the show should go next Saturday. It's probably not fair of me to ask you to inform them but I just don't think I can today. Here's the schedule I would like." He said as he handed his friend a sheaf of papers.

With a startled nod, Luther turned to go. The band wouldn't like making big changes in the show so near concert time never mind getting up the day after.

"Will do, Chance. I'll see you then in a few. Remember this is Andy Devlin of MTV so get your talking hat on." He closed the door quietly behind him, seeming to know there was nothing more to say. This must be big.

Normally the day of a rehearsal this meeting would be short. He'd set the time for their arrival at the venue then bid them a good afternoon.   Not today, he was afraid. They were all present as he entered. Big Dave sat idly drumming a new beat on his I-Pad, Randall was nodding off next to his sax, Pete very busy knocking out a tune on the YAMAHA keys, and as usual, Chuck was alone in a corner plunking away on a new rhythm for his bass. Chet and the band's four man set-up crew sat together playing a game of poker.

"OK, you bunch of losers." Luther said to the assembled group. "Our beloved leader has made a few changes for the show next week, and I'm the one to make the ask. Before you moan and groan, no, I don't know why he wants this but it seemed pretty important to him. It doesn't appear to me that it would be too difficult but you'll have to decide. Please feel free to take notes if needed, Chet, but I also have a printed schedule for all of you." With that, Luther described the new set-up for Saturday night the 25th, and waited for the clamor.

"The last show went Ok but Chance is convinced that it would be best to make a few changes for the one next Saturday. I know it's late in the day but he trusts you guys to be able to adjust." Luther then picked up the sheaf of papers he'd set on the table. "Let's see, we'll start

71

with your song, Bruce. The one we did in January. Remember? The show begins with one bright spot on you and your sax with the rest of us in the background. You get 3 minutes and then Hawk will be lighted on the bass, Dave on the drum, each of you getting three minutes or more if the audience hangs in. Keep an eye on Bruce. He'll signal if this one needs to end. We'll take in the applause, and then we light up Chance. He'll introduce us and how great it is to be there etc. then the song we turned out last year can be the basic piece. It's sold millions already and I know this concert is being recorded. We should be well into an hour by then, I'd say. At this point, we'll go with that new one you wrote in March, Dave. It's much more up to date and even Doja Cat is covering it.

"Anyway, with bows and maybe a short intermission, depending on the attitude of the crowd, that should take us to a couple of hours and Chance would like us to end this gig by highlighting a song which means more than we can imagine to him, I guess. You know what that is, I'm sure. We're to jam it to bits; maybe 30-40 minutes or so. What do you think? He'd like to hit you boys with a rehearsal for this by Monday."

"Geez, Luther. That'll give us a week or so left before we go on and he wants big changes?" offered Dave. "That damn last song would need a big work-over."

"I don't know, Luther. There are only 3 chords of so in that Sunshine thing. Do you think we can milk it for 15 minutes each? On top of that, I'd say the transitions will be a pretty complicated thing but..." Chuck put in.

"What the hell is this anyway? Right at the last minute he expects us to pull a miracle off? This is nuts, if you ask me!" growled Randall.

"Aw for God's sakes guys." said Pete. "Has Chance ever really done anything like this before? I for one, think it might be a colossal finale to our tour this year. With some thought I guess I could come up with somewhere near 64 bars. Maybe a minor key would work."

"How about you, Chet? Would your crew be able to diagram the needs of the band for this by Wednesday for a rehearsal? I really hate to gamble on the last night of our tour but maybe the crowd will like hearing something really new. Maybe even the critics will appreciate such a change." Luther said to the group then gave them a good fifteen minutes to make a decision.

"If it's OK with you guys I'd like to go over and tell him that you're into this and that you will work it out for a rehearsal by Monday, that'll be June 20, at 11. I'd say let's make it at least a 20 minute section for each of you. We will not bother with a rehearsal today and will plan others depending on how Monday goes. And by the way, he also wanted me to ask you to be at the studio in Newbury by noon on the Sunday after the gig, that's June 26. No ideas what for so don't push me."

"He left hearing the grumbling and muttering behind him. He was sure they were up to the challenge. It was his friend he was worried about.

Chance came back from the interview and fell into his Lazy-Boy. It had gone pretty well he thought. There didn't appear to have been any trick questions and he thought the MTV audience would be happy with it. He took a look around the place where he was to be spending his last night of the tour-probably his last night doing anything. Quite possibly, he'd be back behind bars by a week after Monday, July 5th or shortly thereafter. In the meantime he took stock of the venue.

Gillette was bigger than most. It could seat 64,000 regulars with an added 5,876 club seats, and 89 luxury boxes. It was a sell-out within an hour of the band's announcement last August, that their latest tour would include the Boston area.

His guitars hung in just the correct order across the back wall. They started with his electric favorite, his and Chet Atkins' Gibson J40. He felt that would work best for this particular performance. Next in line was the oldest and loudest, a David Gilmour MARTIN D-35. The D-35 was the one he had used for their top selling album.

He had not been able to resist and had decided that the last set would end with the acoustic-the D35 Mother had brought him years ago. He had learned flamenco with that one under circumstances he was yet to face, but he intended to play it Saturday, loud and clear. How he loved those instruments, he thought. Without thinking, he picked up the acoustic and launched into the first tune he had learned, YOU ARE MY SUNSHINE. He then added BESOME MUCHO and broke into tears. This couldn't continue he knew.

"Quit when you're ahead, Chance. You've got fish that need frying." He announced to himself as Luther stepped in. "It's time for us to get on with it."

"Jeesus, Chance." Luther began. "The guys agreed to do their best but I still wonder if you think this is a good idea so late in the game? They've agreed to put something together this afternoon with a rehearsal Monday. You could still change. This Saturday thing is a big night you know; top wages for us all. There's bound to be some prominent Boston critics here. Are you sure the band can afford to take this gamble?"

"Yes! This has been a long 14 month tour and I say let's make the seats rattle. You know what? I don't think I care. I feel I need this. I..." his breath was coming in giant gasps. "I'll try to explain in a minute. As for the guys, did you get Chet to agree with the new stuff? Have you made sure old Weinstein is doing the tracks? Who knows? If this works, this could be the best-selling album we've ever released. It's time to get crazy, I think."

Luther nodded and started to continue discussing it further but could see there was more to come so sat back and waited.

"Okay, that's not all. We'll need to talk a bit now. Would you like to order some food? Or, maybe go somewhere?" He felt himself losing control. "Christ, Luther. I have to do this. Make yourself a drink and just sit down. This will take a lot of long minutes."

Luther turned ashen. The seriousness of the situation took away his ability to speak. Ever since he and Chance had met in that long ago military school, he'd never even seen him flinch at any situation. He had never heard Chance even raise his voice, let alone so hysterically. Not even when he was wounded in Desert Storm. What in the world could this be?

"Sorry Chance. What can I do for you? What's going on? I can stay as long as you need." With that he settled in the other over-stuffed chair in the room and let his friend gather himself.

Nearly 15 minutes went by as Chance wrestled with whatever demons he knew. Then he began.

"I guess the only way to handle this is to barge right in. You know, of course, this is for your eyes only. I won't take a chance on telling my story to the boys. It's too much responsibility to ask them to take on; for you as well, maybe. Feel free to stop me at any time Luther. As you will see, there could be severe consequences if what I'm about to say became public."

Seeing his friend nod spurred him on.

"I am not at all who you think I am. In fact I suppose I could be one of the best phonies you have ever known. My real or do they say original name is not Chance; it's Gertz. Well no, that's not true either. My real name was Middleton I guess." Luther, seeing his friend in such hurt, made a motion to stop him.

"Listen, my man, you don't have to do this. Your background doesn't matter to me. Your friendship has been all I needed for years, you know that. Let's call it for now and maybe with some sleep you'll be better able to make whatever decisions you need. Here" he said handing Chance a glass of scotch. "Give this a try and we'll head for home."

"No way, Luther, I've been hung up on this for way too long as it is. I can't tell you how, but all of a sudden I feel the need to fix some things. Age maybe..." He shook his head to clear his thoughts and began again.

"I don't know who my real father was. I'm not sure my mother ever knew either. It seems I was the product of a wayward young girl in

Hartford, CN; a druggie paying for her fix with the only thing she had to offer, I'm told. Well, not told but discovered by a detective I've hired. It's an old story these days. Her mother wasn't well and couldn't help her and so rather than place me up for adoption, by the time I was three years old her mother, my grandmother, volunteered to raise me. Well, that lasted until she got cancer in her old age and then it gets really complicated."

He seemed to lose his place in the tale and Luther let the silence take over the room. Suddenly with a grimace and a look of hate he had never seen on his friend's face, he began again.

"Let's move on a few years. I had been happy with my Grammy. I was now in fourth grade, had made a few buddies, and she and I got along fine. She hadn't even backed off when she first met me. Imagine Luth, what a shock she must have had on or first meeting. There she was a gray haired single white woman, living on Social Security, planting roses in her small front yard, when her granddaughter arrives and plunks down the likes of me! I was a scrawny, shiny-skinned black boy of 3 years old. I swear I heard her stop breathing. I don't know maybe the blond curls set her off but she gathered herself without hesitation. She took my hand and that was it for the next nine years." Luther reached over and placed his hand on his friend's shoulder.

"C'mon, Chance. You don't have to relive this. Let's get something to eat. I can order whatever you'd like." He said as he grabbed his phone.

"No way; I'm too far into this now. I have to lay it out there to see if my solution might work. Essentially, I was twelve years old when all of my life fell to shit. Suddenly, around the first of November, 1984, there was my grandmother's niece looking me over and making whispered arrangements. In my wildest dreams I could never have imagined how my life would change almost immediately. Gram could no longer care for me. She was ill it seemed. I could be put into an orphanage or I could go live with Aunt Gladys in a small town in NH; Branfield to be exact.

What did I know? I was just a kid. Gladys didn't look too bad. Not pretty like so many of the women we see at our gigs, but sort of strong and she had brought a couple of gifts for me so... Let's face it Luth, my choice was already made for me. Within a month, Gladys returned and I was on my way to disaster as it happens."

"It appeared that from the first day I became a possibility, my new caregiver's husband had changed the design of his old house where he and Gladys would live until the new digs were built. In fact, when I arrived, her new husband, the great Andre Jan Gertz had spent many hours installing a hidden door behind the wine cellar. If one knew which secret button to press they would see a door open and find a room containing a large cage. It took me a minute, but soon I caught on. I was to be kept confined in this cage. I don't know why Gladys didn't realize what was going on during the month before I arrived. I think I remember she seemed shocked at seeing the place I was to inhabit, but not strong enough to change the things he planned.

"For whatever reason, I was to be raised for at least 2 years in that room! That's 24 months!! The place was like a one-room cheap walk-up. One corner of my enclosure was the area where I ate, another for sleeping, and the other for the smelly bathroom with a shower. In addition there was a small desk and chair next to a large bookcase.

"The bars on the room I was to live in were very strong and I recall that with each inch I grew, the height was raised 2 inches. Finally, when I was two years in, the top of the cage was fastened to the bottom of the main floor's 2x 6's. This very effectively kept me from climbing out. I couldn't believe it and I don't think old aunt Gladys could either but she didn't try to help me."

"'Mother Gladys' was around each day around 9AM and brought me the oatmeal and milk that Andre ordered. She appeared not to notice that my confinement was not natural. During those years I think she had been ordered to spend every spare hour she had around her work teaching me to read complicated stuff like Aristotle and Hemingway. He insisted that I write critiques of things I read, and also to manage pretty complicated math. I have kept some of my essays in a bank vault and I must say they were impressive.

"Things I was to discover were ordered by the great Andre Gertz and as it turns out, would be a great help when this nightmare ended and you and I met at HARROW MILITARY ACADEMY.

"As I grew, she would measure me and soon arrive with two new sets of clothes. Whether shoes, trousers, or shirts, all were both black or navy blue, and one size larger than my measurements. In retrospect I now assume that they wanted them to last longer. It didn't matter to me. I was totally at their mercy. Who was going to see me anyway? I ate, I slept, I cried less and less but still...

"My days never varied until I reached the age of 13. On that day, the minute the sun's rays managed to drift in through the small narrow glass of the one slit of window outside my cage, there was good old Andre Jan, my keeper. He entered from a door about 12 feet from my bars. As with every other day, he was dressed in black trousers and wore a white shirt and a checked tie. His voice labored from behind his thick black beard which often caught in the button holes of the gray jacket he wore. He always wore a soft-looking black hat with a crease across the top. I could see his equally black hair which seemed flat against his head and a pair of steely blue eyes. I remember that he had a gold ring on his left hand and wore high-topped shiny black boots. His large hooked nose made me have nightmares in which an eagle, like the one I had seen in the NATIONAL GEOGRAPHIC he required me to read each month, clawed and picked my body to death.

"Well, I was 13 years old..." Chance hesitated. He looked as if he couldn't continue. Luther was alarmed.

"It's OK, my friend. Stop now. You don't have to go on. I've heard enough for a lifetime. Here, let's have a coffee and watch the sun come up. It'll scare all of this away."

"No, I'm afraid not." Chance whispered. "It's time for me to face my demons. The thing is, my friendly keeper made an

78

announcement that I didn't really understand. That morning he came in right on the dot of 9am.

"'Paul come here.' He said. 'I have something to tell you. It's very important. As you know, I am not your real father, Paul, and my wife Gladys is in fact your aunt. She would like very much to be your mother. We know who your mother is but can't find her and as for your father, who knows? Apparently, your blond hair and black skin are in some way connected to your father. My research indicates that he must have been from the Melanesian Islands in the Pacific. You want to hear the bottom line? I think that in spite of your heritage I could make you into a good man. Right now, you are in our charge. So, we would like to ask you if you would mind if we adopted you. If we did, you could call us Mother and Father and we'd take care of you forever.'

"I thought maybe Gladys would be happier if this happened. Maybe I'd be able to go outside the gray door and see some of the things I'd read about. Maybe I could go back to school. And so, I nodded my head.

"Within a month, Andre made his usual entrance but sat down and began, 'Paul Richard Gertz, you are now my son. Someday you may be more powerful than any god. Someday you could be the one everyone will turn to and bow. Or, you can choose to ignore this opportunity and be as worthless as your mother was. Whatever you become, it will because I have made it so. For now you must learn the ways of the world. Today...' and he walked over and picked up a book from the gray shelves to the right of the cage.

"What I later came to know as algebra, history, geography, philosophy, classical literature and science became my companions. I would have to give him this; he is one smart son-of-a-gun and I did learn a great deal.

"Every day Father would stay for exactly three hours, 6 am to 9am, with no break for food or rest. When the sun reached the top of my window he would announce what I should study for the next day. Then he'd pile some books on the little table next to the bed, step from the cage, lock the door and put the rest of the books back on the darkly shadowed shelves. At that, dear old dad disappeared through the basement's heavy gun metal door without a word of goodbye.

"I've asked myself over and over why I didn't balk at his orders, or whine, or maybe just throw a fit. I have no answers other than that I had no one that I thought even knew where I was let alone helping me. At least if I did what he ordered, I hoped I might stay alive.

"As Father left, Mother would soon arrive from some black recess to his left and place food in my cage. As was the way with all of the bizarre action of my life, it too was always the same: a bowl of oatmeal, two glasses of milk, and an orange. Lunch would arrive at 12:30 exactly, (I believe when she took lunch at the town hall). Always the same: a peanut butter and jelly sandwich made with what I think now must have been whole wheat, a large glass of milk, accompanied by an apple. I did not see Father again each day but Mother did return with supper at 5:30: baked beans, cooked cabbage, and a leg of chicken; always boiled, always accompanied by two chocolate cookies. Oh, I forgot to mention, each of them had keys to my room as well as to my cage. Other than the educational stuff, neither of them ever spoke or showed any interest in my well-being or health. That's quite odd, isn't it?

"I have never been able to look at any of those books or foods in the last 30 or so years." Chance said almost with a grin.

"Mother, seldom spoke." he uttered through clenched teeth, "She seemed to be afraid that she would startle herself, but by the second year of my confinement, each day as she picked up the metal bowls, she'd stand outside the bars, her faded blue eyes as wide as saucers. Her voice came out of the dark like that of the most beautiful of birds I had been listening to on the tapes Father had brought in lately. She left me each evening with the same farewell:

'You are my life, Paul. You are not alone. Soon all will change.'

The tones were like the bell that I had heard from the other world outside. The word JOY wasn't known to me then but for some reason my whole body filled with hope and expectation when I heard it. As I grew older and more well-read I would tell myself: 'This must be joy. Perhaps love. Should I feel it as well?'

"The words were barely audible and I believed them less and less as time crawled on.

"I know I was just a kid, but still I noticed that as the months wore slowly by her appearance changed. One day she arrived and I almost didn't recognize her. Suddenly her hair was blonde and clipped somehow at the shoulders. In addition, her lips had red paint on them. She was wearing a pale blue fitted outfit that was knee length and had jewelry on her ears! Another day she came in dressed in something I had seen in the LIFE magazines Andre had supplied. She was wearing trousers just like Andre did! They were white with a black and red block-like design and were topped with a pretty white sweater. Something was happening to her and I began to worry if it would affect me. Would she desert me? Did she care anymore? Every time she left for those first two and a half years, I went back to bawling for an hour or so.

"I have never wept like that again." Chance spoke through his sobs. "Until now, that is. Now tears are a constant in my life."

"One day, October 17, when I'd just marked the year 1985 on the calendar near my desk, I realized that I was growing into a man. For some reason I felt tall and strong and wondered if I could somehow figure a way out of the metal compound. I decided to think up a plan. I had asked for and received a set of encyclopedia and had become a skillful researcher. I found I was pretty good at drawing as well and I spent hours dating and describing in pictures, the days of my life and the two people in it. The outside world became more and more real with each day. I was making notations in the little notebook I kept inside the straw mattress when Mother appeared nearly an hour early."

"She said, 'Paul my dear son, I have a special gift for you today. I know you are probably very angry with me and I hope this present will help make your time pass more pleasantly.' She said as she laid a large leather case on my bed. 'Go ahead and open it. I'm hoping it will make your days go by faster. I don't know a lot about musical instruments but I was told a guitar like this was easy to learn.'

'I haven't much time today as I must get back to work but there's an instruction book in the case to go with it. I think you may want to find a place to hide it...maybe behind your latrine...somewhere where he will not notice it. I think it will give you joy and maybe even happiness. Remember what I say. It will not be long now before all things will change.' "Mother spoke, softly. Like a shadow, she was gone."

"It wasn't long before the D35 became my salvation," Chance added. "As you have guessed, she had given me the Gibson I've been playing for many wonderful years."

"I'm speechless, Chance. I have no idea what to say now." Luther said gently. He arose and placed his arm across his friend's shoulders. "What can I do to ease the pain? Is it enough just to have someone else to carry the burden? If so, I'm OK with that. I..."

"No. Luther. I need to fix it. I believe that I can't just let go. I know you may even hear of this whole thing getting messier and so I wanted you clear of it. I plan on just telling the boys that I can't go on and have some things to work out. They're all grown-ups and I hope they will forgive me. By the way, I've met a woman who matters. She may not tolerate my solution but...we'll see."

He rose and clasped his friend to his chest then added, "There probably is no lawful justification for my future actions. Stay out of this if approached, Luth. I'll see you Monday at the rehearsal and let's hope the crew will be OK for Saturday." He said as he held the door for his friend. "I will be ready to let the boys know somehow when we meet in Newbury on Sunday after the concert."

"You are one crazy son of a bitch, Chance." Luther said as the door closed behind him.

As one would expect from such a seasoned and talented crew, the rehearsal and the following concert went without a hitch. In fact, the last set nearly overwhelmed the crowd. Critics and TV broadcasters who were there couldn't say enough about show especially the finale.

As asked, The Stragglers had taken a three chord song, YOU ARE MY SUNSHINE, written by Jimmie Davis, and whipped the crowd into a frenzy. The arrangement of this simple song included each member of the band taking fifteen to 20 minutes to show what originality and talent can do with any melody. Drummer Dave set out with a slow, steady beat and then warped it into a Latin flavored jazz riff. Then Pete took over on his keyboard making one believe Dave Brubeck had never touched an ivory. Chuck soon added a wailing bass a la the now popular India sound, Bollywood. With each added bit, the crowd seemed to become more involved and by the time Rand finished adding chord progressions on top of the simple basic chords of the song, nearly 60,000 people were stomping, clapping in rhythm, Gillette could be heard for miles.

Then suddenly, the stage went dark except for one bright spot focused on Chance; sitting at the front of the stage, alone on an old wooden chair. The single spot caught in his blond hair and his guitar. He had changed his outfit and now wore only jeans and a light blue tee. His signature wide-brimmed hat hung loosely from a rawhide string. The crowd seemed to know what he needed; dead silence fell over the arena. For a few minutes, he held the old acoustic guitar gently in his arms and then began. Notes fluttered through the air, then whirled form the strings. Those nearest the stage would later swear that they saw tears flowing down his cheeks. Fifteen minutes later, he stood and took a bow, then gestured to the band members to do the same. Silence remained. For nearly five minutes thousands of patrons stood in awe.

As Chance gathered his old guitar and started off the stage, a lone female voice began to sing. 'You Are My Sunshine, My only Sunshine'...Within seconds another voice joined her and on and on it went until the words and the simple tune filled the air.

Nearly twenty minutes later Luther ambled on to the stage and expressed the band's thanks. He then stood next to Chance, the lights were dimmed, and Chance and the Stragglers left.

The reaction was immediate. Before the new album could even be released, the critics were crowning it as the best of the decade, probably destined to be a classic of the twenty first century. The accolades were spread to each member of the band and then heaped on that of Chance for what they called a genius arrangement.

The next day the band members gathered still full of pride and excitement. They expected to see their leader the same. Chance was brief.

"I'm so proud of what we have accomplished, guys. Not only will our music be popular for many years, but each and every one of you will be able to call whatever shots you desire. As for me, I would imagine you have sensed that I have not been myself for quite a while. You were not mistaken. I'm so sorry to have to tell you, that last night will need to be my last performance for the foreseeable future.

"I have a personal problem that cannot be put aside. I need to address it soon. I want you to go ahead and find another leader or just hang up for a while and see how this plays out. There will be no more discussion on my part as I want you to be kept out of the loop as this thing develops. My thanks and love to you all. Be happy."

With that Luther took his friend's arm and they left the room.

CHAPTER VI

JESSIE'S

Morris sat quietly in the corner. The light from the dimly lit bar hardly touched his face. He liked that. In fact, he loved the feeling of anonymity here in Greenview. The whole scenario brought peace to his mind; faceless, unchallenging peace. It didn't even seem as if Jessica had noticed he was here, but of course she had. The three mugs of beer appeared, every 20 minutes or so without a sound; MODELO with just a bit of foam. With each he nodded his thanks-with the third offered his twenty dollars. They both knew it was an extravagant tip but their rankling had ceased a year ago. She quietly scooped up the money, whispered a thank you and moved away.

The regulars were still sitting in their habitual places...Harry on the outside, Jack in the middle, Adam to his left. One could always tell time here, watch or none. At six-o-clock they sat boldly straight tapping on the marble deck before them every few minutes and throwing a buck and change down upon the new mug's arrival, By now though their spines had acquired the curved look of a weary traveler or maybe even the men he had seen putting away shovels after working a long day of post-digging. Not one of them would be home on time. Morris grimaced a bit as he thought of the Friday night discussions that would surely be coming to these guys. Wives and mothers wait-especially on pay day, he thought. Friday night was the time to add up their earnings, make decisions about where it was to be spent and then eke out a bit for a special Saturday treat. At least he had observed that. He had had no personal experience to back the thought up but did know that when he returned on Saturday night at least two of the trio would be absent, and by Sunday he would see them with family in tow, heading up the stairs of St. James Episcopal as he looked up from his Sunday Times. He never went further with his observations...it was still too painful.

This night appeared to be different, though. As he adjusted his thick, tinted glasses he noticed the three had become closer, heads together, conspiratorial, maybe. He could make out a piece of paper or maybe it was a tablet. He couldn't quite see without gawking. The thing had appeared on the bar before them and all three seemed very interested in it. Whatever it had to do with them obviously was big he thought. He could tell by the shaking of heads and incredulous looks that appeared. He would say that Adam was the perpetrator of their discussion and he was glad. As suddenly as it had appeared it disappeared into thin air and with great serious handshakes the three struggled off to find their ways home. Well, that was out of the ordinary, but promising, he thought.

A couple more hours went by quickly. It was time. It was 10pm. It was time for him to go. With a silent nod to Jessica, he stood, carefully buttoned the black suede overcoat, placed his black hat brim shading his eyes, and left by the back door.

"Who in the world was this guy?" The owner remarked to herself. "A whole year and I still don't think anyone in this town could tell me. Well, I don't dare to ask. I'll be the "new person" in this small berg for another ten years. No one would be interested and they'd swear I was just filling in my time with gossip." Something to ruminate about anyway, she thought. With that, she was off to welcome a group just coming in from seeing Tom Hanks' newest movie.

By 1AM she had served "Last Call", collected monies owed, and ushered the group out the door. She set to her nightly cleaning routine but could not seem to shake thoughts running through her mind. She, too, had noticed her three regulars very seriously studying the paper or some kind of tablet that Adam Rollins had laid on the counter. Just taking in their fascinated perusal gave her the impression of its importance. What in the world? These guys were hard working stiffs she'd known for the whole four years she'd owned the place. Other than the occasional argument about a Bruin's game as they gawked at the local newspaper she'd never seen them read anything of substance.

"Must be important." She muttered aloud.

It was obvious it wasn't to be shared with anyone else in the place, that's for sure. In fact Adam had kept his voice to a whisper and his hand shielding the tome from any wandering eye. Hmmm. What a night; first the ghost man and then these three with their big secret.

Well, she thought. That's that for Saturday June17, 2022. Suddenly she was exhausted. She wondered if all tavern owners got this tired. Tomorrow was Sunday she reminded herself. She'd have time to herself if she played her cards well.

For no reason she immediately decided to call her mom in Camden. Helen didn't ever sleep. This would be a good time-right after the late news before she would hit the sack

"Hi Mom." She said after one ring. "How was your day? Are you feeling OK?"

"Why Jessie you call at the worst time I must say." snapped the familiar voice. "I'd just finished my wine and was hitting the sheets. To what do I owe this late night call?" the familiar puff following her words.

"Ah yes, I can hear you're back to smoking Mom. I was so hoping you'd walk away from it this year. Do you ever pay any attention to your doctors?" Catching herself, she began again, "Sorry, I didn't really want anything other than to hear your voice and catch up a bit. They have allowed us to open finally and I have been extra busy here this week. I plan on hiding away somewhere tomorrow. So..."

"I guess that's good." said her mother. "You know how I feel about this project of yours. I was sure you'd end up at a law firm or maybe a big investment place in Boston, or..."

"Mom!" Jessie almost shouted. "Is there no support in your whole system? All I wanted was a nice mother/daughter chat. You know the kind Dr. Phil and the talking heads put out. And Geez! You have to put in the barbs. I...Listen. Let's start over. I'm happy with my decision for now. I like this little town of Grandview. The people generally are friendly and I have established a bit of a reputation for good service. Matter of fact, I think the place will show a profit now that COVID is supposed to be under control by December. They're saying that with masks we'll be able to stay open this time. The year 2022 will be good."

"December??? It's now June! What will you live on for the next few months??? For God's sakes, Jessie! Make a profit?? During a pandemic! You will never cease to amaze me. You were half way through your Doctorate four years ago...people who matter were clamoring for you to work with them. I didn't mind a bit spending your father's money on your future. Well I hope this isn't one of those calls asking for more...have you already used up all of your inheritance?" spewed forth the old mantra.

"Just forget I called, mom. I was a bit weary, I guess. No. I don't need your money but yes, I do love what I'm doing so let's not speak of it again. I'm glad you're OK; with dad gone so suddenly it has to be lonely. Again, I would be happy to have you move up here from Jersey if you would feel more comfortable. All I'm asking is that you think it over. You might even like this town, who's to say?"

"You're right, Jess. I do get a bit testy. I guess I didn't expect my only child to become a bar tender. Look. Let's just stop this. Tonight I'm tired of it. I did hope for more from you but..." with that she hung up. Jessie cried a few tears as she flipped off her cell. What did she expect? Her mother had always been single minded and always right, in her own view at least.

Never give up, she told herself. The call she made was in hopes of mending fences with her. Maybe they could both learn to allow each other some space. Maybe they could be family again. Maybe lions would whisper. Maybe...maybe...maybe.

With that thought she rose and turned off the outside sign and lights, made sure the security locks were set and climbed upstairs to her home. Tomorrow would be here too soon for anymore thinking. The door barely closed before she fell into bed exhausted.

The sun was just up when she awoke. God! Jessie thought. I wanted to sleep late but here I am wide awake and it's only 8AM. Damn. Six hours of sleep never had been enough for her. Maybe her mother was right. What in the world was she doing trying to keep a bar going far into the night?! Wait a minute. Stop Jess! I've mulled this over far too long. This is Sunday; my day of NO thinking. She had been exhausted lately and had conned her cook to hold the fort for this day. She opened one eye and glanced at the clock. Is this too late? I can still get a few winks. With a tap on the alarm button she headed off to dream land.

Four hours later she awoke with a start. What time is it? Where am I? What day is it? The questions swirled. It took a few minutes to orientate her. I've got to stop working so late she muttered. She beat the clock's button firmly as it dinged its call to arms, then purposefully headed for the Cuisinart and switched it on. Within an hour Jessica had her morning latte in hand and was ready to enjoy what might be left of the day. But first she needed to go through her Sunday ritual: a walk around her home.

She loved her little place and was very pleased with what she had done with the interior. The whole front half had been painted with Chalk white walls throughout. She had added a beige couch and a couple of modern Swedish loungers, a small kitchen/dining area took up the eastern end. All areas were decorated with bold accents of coral, blue and pale mustard pillows, bright bowls, and a few paintings she had bought from a friend years ago. The back third contained her bedroom suite while another room had quickly become a guest/den/work space. It had a second bathroom as well as a Murphy bed. She had turned this place into the privacy one might want and a happy place to entertain. She supposed the present nomenclature would be "female cave". Ugh! She hated that expression for some reason. Why do people insist on labeling everyone and everything today?

The wonderful home, (which was now maybe 10% hers she reminded herself) came to life for her every Sunday. She never could stop reviewing her choice and marveling at the luck that had come her way. Now, as she stepped down the outside stairway she'd had installed immediately upon moving in, she stopped at the landing outside her living area and took it all in.

She could still feel the pull of the place that had materialized just around a New England corner that fall. That day it had seemed as if New Hampshire had dressed itself in the finest of clothes: Yellows, Reds and Oranges never matched by hundreds of artists over the years; a bottom-less blue sky-cloudless and breezy allowing breathless moments for her senses. She wondered whether she could see 100 miles. She'd heard it could be done. Was that Boston in the distance-maybe Crochet Mountain over to her left? Wherever it was, that September day was a day to be revisited in the dreary months of January or February. Grabbing her cell she snapped a few photos to be added to the million or so she already had.

What a tale she had weaved since leaving Columbia in the spring of 2016. She had been distressed-unsure of her future, and then blowing off steam and quitting the whole thing. No. She had decided. She did not want to be a doctor, or lawyer or even a chief of some kind. She needed a spot of her own. One for which only she would be responsible. She was sick of answering to professors, to counselors, to her mother; fed up with New York City. With that she had unlocked her KIA Soul and headed out for who knew??? North seemed OK and before she knew it she was just over the border in New Hampshire somewhere, rounding a corner and confronted by a fancy sign announcing that the business behind it was for sale.

It stood bright and cheery directly in front of a two storied building whose paint job had not seen a brush for some time. Something drew her in and she stopped and parked to one side to get a better view.

A forlorn sign hung at its front entrance stating that they were permanently closed. The letters were nearly obliterated by the grime of years. For who knew what reason it appeared to have been left quite suddenly. Peeking through the front window, she could see a uniform on one chair and a receipt book of sorts lying on the shabby bar. Apparently it had been a restaurant and bar in its day because one could see a long bar with a few high tops in front. There were also chairs atop the a few tables inside. Some bottles had even been left on shelves. She assumed there must be a small kitchen behind the bedraggled swinging doors to the left of the bar. She was unsure why she would have bothered to stop. This place was a mess.

Still she decided to back off and take another look. What had attracted her so much? Well, both floors had wide windows open to vistas unparalleled. A small river across the street grew wider here, making a sharp ninety degree turn after lapping the stone wall barriers containing it. Its two hundred foot width reflected the sky of the day and would frame the much darker stars of the night. Across the river one could see several homes each with docks keeping various sized boats safely moored at their sides. This is beautiful now and I can imagine what it will look like in the spring, Jessie thought, and what a view from that small veranda above the business! Without another minute's hesitation, she found her IPhone and hit the sign's number. By late afternoon weeks later, on September 24, 2016, papers had been signed, monies offered and accepted and she owned a piece of property without knowing what she intended to do with it.

The afternoon after the sale, she found herself sitting alone in the middle of a dust-ridden room staring at a dark stairwell pondering what had hit her. What did she know about running a restaurant or a bar? What else could she do with this disaster? Let's face it she had had to use all of her inheritance, just to own it. It certainly was a long way from the medical or law firms her mother had always imagined for her. With that thought she hit the UNLOCK BUTTON on the KIA, gathered the few belongings she had and headed upstairs with her sleeping bag.

CHAPTER VII

THREE GUYS AT THE BAR

It was Friday night. Adam was free as a bird. JESSIE'S blue neon sign flashed its welcome just around the corner as he sped down route 33. He hit the brakes and slid into his regular place. The Corvette gurgled a bit then settled onto the pea-stone.

They had chosen this particular bar because it was away from Branfield. They really liked Jessie. She could always be counted on for a smile and never seemed to be nosy. Thirty or Forty miles or so wasn't a long drive and they could just hang out and relax. Whew! It's good to be done for the day, Adam muttered as the door swung behind him. The place wasn't very crowded yet and the new eats thing she was trying meant he could tarry longer. He didn't have anybody to answer to but the other two had wives with plans for the end of the week.

He felt really tired for a Friday. Usually he and the boys were ready for slamming down a few and then a raucous time at home. Not this day he thought. I'm too depressed. He was sick and tired of working for his uncles at Rollins Inc. and had just he had quit the job at Gertz Hardware.

It seemed to him that he had much more to offer than just knowing what hammer to buy or showing off his knowledge of paint colors. Geez! Here he was the son of one of the most prominent families in the state of New Hampshire, and all he could find for work was this? Something didn't seem right that's for sure. He probably should have stayed in the Navy. He'd done well and had learned a great deal about coding and digital warfare. He had thought he could parlay this into a good paying job but 3 years of looking and interviewing had not turned up anything. The little side business he had just started had roped in Andre Gertz but that was the only client he had in the last three weeks. He'd thought of trying to work with his dad but just couldn't stand always being told what to do so who knows? He was now newly divorced with an ex and two kids to support. Probably he deserved to be where he was but Geez! He always came to the same conclusion: No ties-that's what he needed. This was the prime of his life. He should be making a lot more money and living it up.

"Hey, Jessie." he said. "How about a BUD tonight? Anything special they're bringing in?"

"Hi Adam. It's good to see you. Where's the other two? I haven't seen any of you for two weeks. Have they given up coming? And no, Bud is the best I've got. You want a can, bottle, or tap?"

"Aw. I'll have a bottle. They're around. Both said they'd be here; probably cashing their checks. The Missus always wants to ... track, you know. They like to get their hands on the green before anyone else. I'll tell you one thing, I'm glad I'm not tethered to the *home fires and babies routine* anymore. Worst thing I ever did was marry that Mary Riley. You hear anything about her lately?"

"Only that she and Dave are maybe going to marry sometime in December." Jessie said as she planted the bottle in front of him. "They seem pretty happy to me." She added. Then moved down the bar wiping it off in advance of the next customer.

Within ten minutes the other members of the crew entered with hearty grabs and greetings. Jack Lemire was her favorite. He always had a smile and looked at the world with an upbeat attitude she thought. She did love that curly-haired Harry Sykes though. What a handsome guy. I wonder why I like blond hair so much, she asked herself.

"Hi guys" she said. "Are we both in for a bottle of Bud?" They nodded and plopped themselves on either side of Adam. They were settling in for a long session tonight

"Well, we might as well dig in." He took a lot of time casing the area around them and then said as he gestured for them to move closer. "I told you I've got this interesting proposition. Came out of the blue on Wednesday night about 11pm. Sort of mysterious but...listen up and we'll see what you guys think."

With that he took out a small black tablet with a page of dates and writing, and began his spiel.

"We talked a bit the other night, but I didn't think we made a decision so I brought more info for you to see. Number 1, I'd say whoever this is has a big pair, and he's willing to shell out a lot of cash for results so keep this way under your hats, guys." He nearly whispered.

Both of the others blanched at his approach. There was nervousness to his voice that alerted his two companions. They had been thinking that Adam had stopped his wild ideas.

"It must be something really monstrous for you to be nervous." whispered Jack.

"I agree. I've never seen you this jumpy before; even when we stole that Jeep to go for that joy ride when we were still at BHS. And, by the way, how come you always come to us when you've got some kind of crooked deal in mind?" offered Harry.

"Hey, Adam, is there any chance you've come up with a legitimate idea this time?"

95

"OK, Adam old man. Get on with it." They said in unison.

With a slug or two from his Bud, Adam told his tale. "So I had just settled down for the long winter's nap, as they say, and Wham! Out of the blue my cell rings. You know how it is when that happens? You're sure it's some kind of emergency, especially when you've got family strewn all around the town. Matter of fact I even began to sweat before I answered. This voice I swear I've never heard before...I think he had muffled it somehow; got right to the point. Let's see, I want to be accurate here..." he added as he opened his tablet. "I don't know why but I grabbed this and hit record so listen carefully."

'I've heard that you are not happy with the work you're doing and would like to offer you a job. This job needs to be very secret. It would even lead to felony charges if you decide to give it a try. You would not need any help but might want some I'd say and they'd need to be more trustworthy than any God I know. Should I go on?'

"I was blown away. Who could this be? How in the world did he know me? And, get my cell number? I never just throw it around! Plus, why would he know I was unhappy with my job? I decided what the Hell. Might as well find out what he wanted so I told him to continue."

'I understand that you have extensive experience at carrying out a job I have. I would like to talk further and will be glad to arrange a private meeting. If you can figure out a way to accomplish what I wish the pay would be 100 grand; half when you start and the other when finished. It would be up to you to decide if you need any help. If you are interested, contact me at THE OLD CROW restaurant in Hartford, CN, on Thursday, June 16 at 8pm. I will know you and will make contact there.'

"As you can hear, this guy sounds very positive and sure of himself so I'd assume he was using a burner phone that couldn't be traced." Adam inserted. "You guys know my dad is still in the police business so I could call him and report this, or I can wait to meet him before making any decisions. Or maybe you have something else. What do you think?"

Silence fell over the trio. Not one of them even went to the bottles in front of them. Ten minutes passed before Jake spoke up.

"A hundred grand??! This guy must be Mafia or something. Who else has that kind of cash lying around, and, why you? For that matter why have you chosen to tell us? Are you really considering this? I think I'd better call it a day. Alice will be waiting and..." He rose to put on his jacket.

"Wait up. Wait up." Harry interjected. "I don't want to hear any more either. This is nuts Adam, and you know it. I'm not thinking about jail any time soon and this surely sounds right up that alley."

"I agree, Adam. Toss those notes and don't ever answer your phone again. In fact I'd advise that you get a new one. Follow his lead and get a burner. I'm gone." Jake grumbled.

As they rose to go, Adam grabbed them both by the arms.

"You might want to hear the rest." He said. "The job needs to be done within the month of June and if anything goes wrong, I'd be given a new name and address in a new state immediately. He plans to contact me within a week for my answer."

"Has it occurred to you," said Jake, "that he's made contact and knows who and where you are?"

"I think we're all in danger here, unless we call the FBI or some such." Harry responded. "Look, Adam, you know I have a wife and kid and I have to say I don't mind my job at the store much at all. In fact, I kind of like people to think I know stuff. I'm thinking its grow-up time for me. I'm giving this a pass."

"Oh, for Christ Sakes Jack. Listen up now. Under no circumstances are you to mention this to anyone else. Do you hear me? Why are you always so cautious? Do you have any idea what I could do with a hundred grand? I'd never have to work again. I could travel around the world." Adam's voice rose as he spoke.

Harry stepped in immediately. "Look guys. Keep your voices down. This sounds very dangerous to me. How in the world could you even be thinking of doing it? Why in the world would anyone want this?? I admit I'm curious but I still say it's best to let it lie. Are you sure you're smart enough to pull it off? I'm kind of fond of my life right now and as you guys know, I never have been a gambler. Let's order another brew and talk about the Sox. It looks like this will be their year."

With that, Adam closed his tablet, put it in his pocket and got up to go.

"OK boys. If that's the way you want it. But I'm interested. We'll see if he contacts me again. I tell you what, if he calls and I think it's legit, do you want me to let you know?"

Jake and Harry shook their heads and added a resounding "No!" then left. Adam took the time to put money on the bar and headed for his car. Not one of them noticed the odd man in the corner talking to Jessie.

OK. So, that's an idea that's down the drain, thought Chance. Probably shouldn't have even tempted him. Maybe I should ask Luther for help. Perhaps there's someone else.

Panic took over his thoughts. He began to sweat. Well, well, well. Perhaps I don't have the cajones for this kind of thing. With that, he pulled his brim down, buttoned the long coat and headed for the door. This whole thing needed more thought. No, dammit. It doesn't, and I know it. I know exactly what I should do. This is my rodeo, my risk, and I have no right to involve anyone else. It's get off the pot time, old man, and the one man who needs to be doing so is driving this car.

In four days he arrived at exactly 8PM at THE OLD CROW. Once he ordered, a beer and burger he took time to look the place over. There in a corner booth sat his man of the hour. Two weeks later, the vaunted Mayor of Branfield, NH, issued a terse announcement to his supporters and disappeared.

NOTICE: Mayor Andre Jan Gertz and Gladys Gertz, your town clerk, will be out of town on personal business until the end of July. Any communications can be sent to: Robin at Hunter@Google.com

With a smile, Adam Rollins quietly left town to see the world.

The town was ablaze with gossip. They had all seen the note; it had been published in the local Journal, after all. In fact most had a copy stuffed in a pocket.

"So, what do you think?" asked Jenny of her daughter over morning coffee at BETTY'S. "Kind of unusual at the least I'd say."

"Oh, for gosh sakes, mom, give them a break. Apparently, they have had some kind of private thing happen and it requires their attention. Big deal!" exclaimed Alice. "I'll bet it might be some kind of vacation to regroup. I wish I had the dough to take one. Guaranteed they'll be back bright eyed and bushy-tailed, ready to run the town again. And by the way, I predict no one will even notice they're gone."

She was correct. Within a week no one even asked about the Andre Jan Gertz. They had other more pressing issues than a vacation trip. Chance had bet correctly.

CHAPTER VIII

CONCLUSIONS & CONNECTIONS

Throughout the months Martha had found a way to post large lettered notes on the glass that surrounded Dennis' bed so he knew that the boys had found a way to stay afloat and keep their restaurant open even the face of COVID. They had tightened up their hours lessening the times they were open for business inside and had established a better staffed take-out crew. Almost all of their menu could now be either delivered or picked up at the drive-thru tent they had placed in the parking lot. The arrangement even allowed them to keep most of their servers working if they wished. It had taken time to train order takers and help pack the take-out boxes but as of the summer of 2022 they were solvent.

Dennis had also survived the worst. He was to be removed from the breathing machine this week. He was to be released on June 5, 2022, all things being equal. She was ecstatic. He was worried that she might be expecting too much. He had written about what a chore it would be to get his throat working again and hoped Martha wasn't thinking it would only take a day or two. He said he'd had patients who were still experiencing hoarseness and weakness for six months or so after they were released from the hospital.

Typical of Dennis, she thought. He said he had been trying to compose a letter of apology to her for some time. Nothing appeared to be enough to neutralize the colossal mistake he had made by not making the time to get his shots. Nearly a year had now passed and the time he had spent ignoring his family seemed insurmountable. Now with recovery there would be a few months more before he could make amends. He told her that the debt he owed his wife and sons, was overwhelming.

"Oh come on my dear." Martha said gently into the phone. "You have done a wonderful job for our townspeople and I'm so glad you're coming home. The word forgiveness shouldn't even enter our minds. Let's just roll with the punches and get you back on your feet. The kids will be so happy to show you the grandchildren. This is going to be great. Nowhere near as futile as the last few months have been." She added.

Suddenly, Martha's realized the house phone was ringing. "My God! Will it never end?" She mumbled as she picked it up.

"Hi Marth." said Marion. "I know this isn't Wednesday but I was going a bit stir crazy. I probably shouldn't have retired so early. The day whizzed by then. I was so busy teaching and prepping to teach, weeks seemed like a minute. How are you doing? How about we get together a bit early this week and could you make it today?"

"I guess I'm OK but I feel very crazy today." answered Martha. "Aw, why not? I am anxious to talk about our work and I bet Tavia is too. What in the world is this thing you're doing anyway?"

"Well. I'm in the middle of a dilemma. I can't believe I'm saying this but I'm in the process of going through old BHS yearbooks I collected. I decided I had no idea why I was keeping them. Do you remember all of our classmates? I must have had my nose really stuck up that's all I can say. For some reason I thought that Gladys Medford was just a bit behind us but it turns out she was 10 years behind. My lord. This set me to thinking more about our latest mayor.

He went to school here too, you know. One Andre Jan Gertz was born in 1945 and graduated in 1963. He sure has kept himself in shape, I'd say: kudos to Doris and her friends. Do you know him or Gladys well? I must admit I only know what I read in the papers and of course what I've read from our research. Ten years was a lot when we were teens and they would both have gone off to school even before we graduated so..." Marion rattled on.

"My gosh, Marion, what a wondrous thing for you to be doing. I don't think I even have a saved yearbook or much of anything else in the way of souvenirs. I only remember being glad we were friends and very interested in one Dennis Haltson most of the time. My mother was on my back to play the field more but I didn't go for that idea at all. Do you think there is such a thing as love at first sight, or is it just easier to choose and not have to play the field?" queried Martha.

"Well, that worked for you two." said Marion. I remember it was hard to get an hour or two with you alone for girl talk. I guess I didn't do too well. I was so anxious to get out of the house and have a family that I fell for the first fellow who flattered me a bit. As I look at all of the guys now I can see a better choice or two but one look at Bill Heron and his shiny blue Chevy and I guess I was blind to them all. Ah well. I've been very lucky as it happens. I have my two kids grown and successful and now a couple of grandchildren to spoil and I have Hal. How do I deserve to be so happy?"

"I don't know, Mare, but this seems like a great day to nurture this conversation. Let's give Octavia a buzz and see if she'd brave enough to have lunch here. I'm still not going into restaurants because Dennis says it's far too dangerous. He should know. And did I tell you they he'll be off the ventilator this month-with luck back home in a few weeks." Martha said happily.

103

Marion could hear the smile on her face. "That's great news. OK, I'm calling Tavia." She added.

Octavia was glad to go with the suggestion and by 11:30 the three old friends sat in Marion's sunny den, paging through the old days. Once again they got side-lined as they discussed their long ago classmates and as expected, Octavia's conquests.

"Oh, yeah. That's John Cleary. We had the best time at the sophomore dance. He married Harriet Plummer you know. Geez. Look at Henry Blandings. He wasn't too bad looking and he and I had great times swimming at the lake in the summer of '70. He's a lawyer now, you know. Not married either. Hmmm. And good old Bill Ryan, remember him? He and I were homecoming King and Queen in '71. I probably missed a good guy that time but he kind of bored me."

"Octave, will you ever change? Let's see, you tried 3 for real since all of these good old days and now I hear you and our most eligible bachelor the police chief are on the outs. What happened?" said Martha.

"Well, I really like him and he's a wonderful catch but I just couldn't deal with the way he has raised his kids. Not all of them. The Virginia is OK; married and happy. But that Adam is spoiled rotten and I don't trust him a bit. I know he doesn't like me either. He's been able to pull the wool most of his life. Jimmy is always hauling him out of some mess and we have had some unfortunate battles about that. I've always had the feeling that he'd do some damn thing that he couldn't be extricated from and I've warned and warned but Jim will never change. I need to move on with Jimmy or just live the rest of it as a single."

"Yes. Hal said that Adam had been a problem. He's 33 now, you know. He said that both he and Jim really liked Mary Riley and had hopes but Adam couldn't keep his eyes off every girl that passed so she dropped him. Too bad. On the other hand do you think there are just some men or women for that matter, who just won't change?" Marion asked.

"I'm sure I wouldn't be one to give advice on people's behavior, but I do think we need to get on with whatever research we've done and get back to a better understanding about the Gertz and Branfield." said Octavia.

They all agreed and took out the original notes they had made, ready to add any necessary information to Marion's report. Octavia had had many talks with her and Gladys' old friend Julie as well as some of the old friends she saw at her museum. Marion had been able to delve into the old town files at the school as well as those in the Branfield Historical Society. Martha had struck a gold mine when she realized that one of her friends' cousins, Nancy Hall, had been involved in helping Gus raise Andre. It turned out that she and another of the neighbors, Susan Elliot had taken turns babysitting for the boy for nearly 10 years.

They couldn't resist talking about what they had found. All announced that they had not felt ready to tell their husbands or friends what they had done, but felt that if they decided to go further, they'd need to remedy that.

"Egad!" said Martha. "I feel like a gossipy old woman. There's no way Dennis would appreciate this. I'm telling you right now, as long as I've lived and as jaundiced as I am as far as the world goes, I'm still blown away."

"I know what you mean." answered Octavia. "I've heard that everyone can find out every secret you have but I doubted it. No more."

"Yes, well. I'd say you we proved that. But, have we accomplished anything?" said Marion. "What was it you proposed, Octavia? Can we get to know the Gertz better? Do we care? What do you two think now?"

"You know, I was interested in the family story. They were so in love and made such a great beginning and then...Wham! The rug disappeared. Not a new happening but it surely took its toll. One of the things that I forgot to include was Andre's self-centered personality. More than once I had someone insinuate that one shouldn't let him or

105

herself get on his wrong side. I heard that from all five of the neighbor women who helped raise him. Each one said they tried to get him to deeply care about others but felt he paid no attention unless it would benefit him." Martha put in.

"I felt that Gladys became no more than a step on his ladder. You know. There she was, a good daughter and employee, when at a very vulnerable middle age along came what he wanted her to see: Pope Pius himself." Marion said in agreement. "When I finished typing all of our notes I really had no idea if she had ever been happy. But there they are, living in the most luxurious home in Branfield, and probably waltzing in to the senate and the position of mayor. Wow!"

"I agree with you Mare. However, I felt every time I interviewed any of the town's politicians some were not quite sure if this was the way to continue running our town. They seemed to be uncomfortable with nepotism and I agree." Octavia threw in.

"Oh, I don't know. The older ones seem pretty happy with their elite community. I did notice that younger people were less so, not that there are many. By the way, the stuff you learned about Gladys from Julie was hair-raising. Whatever do you think happened to her nephew? He'd be well into his 40's now. I hope it worked out for him." Marion offered.

It took nearly two hours for the three to reiterate their findings. At that point they had covered all of the distance from the family's immigration to Andre's rise to success in the small town, to the gossip about his marriage to Gladys and his election as their mayor. With very little exception they accepted Marion's version of the whole thing.

"It's Andre and Gladys Gertz we started out to examine and I'd say we certainly aren't able to say that either of them should be drummed out of the town." said Martha. "But I still have this feeling. Why has Andre and his supporters been so bent on making our town just a high class bedroom town? Is there money passing hands? I have to admit I haven't found anything illegal..."

"As far as I'm concerned, Gladys would be OK as a mayor but I just don't trust Andre. I think he's always been only helpful for himself and his cronies." said Marion. "Now is probably the time for us to revisit Octavia's big news. Do we want Andre to be our senator? Will Gladys make a good mayor? Do they have enough clout to be elected? I tell you what, we're lifetime residents of Branfield and we have the time to care about its future. I'm inclined to think that the best way to know what to do would be to go to the source. I know they've holed up at the mansion, apparently to decide what their future will look like. How about next week we make it a point to find out if we can get an interview and pay them a visit? Is that too extreme?" Octavia said absently.

"Oh, and by the way, the other night, Jimmy and I went out to a new place called JESSIE'S, Down by the border, and guess what? There in the corner sat the guy that people have been seeing around town; black hat, coat, and all. I mentioned it to Jimmy again and he felt the description of the man who bought the old Gertz homestead was just what we were seeing. He's been making it a habit to cruise around the town and have friendly conversations with newcomers and thought he'd include that place and see if this guy turned up. Who knows? Maybe he'll find out who this guy is. Do you suppose he's got something to do with the Gertz?"

"That's a heavy suggestion and I'm too tired to think about it. Stranger things have happened, I guess. Well, that's more than enough for today I say." offered Martha. "I'd bet the Gertz couple are just relaxing at the manor. Let's give it a few days then talk again. I need a nap."

The three agreed and headed for home unaware of the real facts. The details would have astounded them.

CHAPTER IX
PAUL RICHARD MIDDLETON
aka
MORRIS GEORGE CHANCE

The afternoon was waning and Morris decided it would be best not to take any more chances of recognition. He'd wandered around Branfield so much he could almost believe he had lived there once. Obviously, his mother was determined to stay. Andre was successful. He had wealth and power. What power he had over her was beyond him at this point but maybe with a beer and a bit of rest something would make sense. Let's face it he told himself, I also have power, wealth, and position if I want it. What more could anyone ask?

By seven-o-clock he had made it to JESSIES. He entered through the side entrance and took his place in the shadows. The question he had asked himself about Andre's behavior still rattled in his brain. Morris grimaced at the fact that he was the one asking such a question. Here he was, Fifty years old and unable to cope with his life's story. He had money. He had fame. He wanted nothing material he could think of. Still, the saga had played its drum in his brain more and more as he moved through life. He had gotten less and less sleep in the past few years. He was unable to concentrate on any meaningful future plans. He was now overcome by nightmares even with the help of the many doctors he had seen.

Jessie arrived just as he was about to smash his fist through her table. She left his third beer, and then moved on without a word. Paul realized that he couldn't just let it go anymore. Somehow, he needed to take up arms as the bard would say, and the sooner the better. He waved Jessie over to his table and started his apology.

"I'm sorry to have been so mysterious. As you might guess, I've been hoping that our relationship might move to something more serious but...do you think it could?" He couldn't look at her face when he asked.

"No. I'm sorry. That's pretty forward of me isn't it? Let me start again. Jessie, I've been coming here off and on for a few months and I was wondering if you'd be interested in dinner or something or...Damn...Am I way off base?"

"Well, well." said Jessie. "All this time and finally you piped up. You know, I've been afraid to make a move, too. You've been so mysterious that...But sure. Let's have a later dinner after I close up tonight. It'll be after ten so I guess HENRY'S over in Methuen would be the only place open. Would that be OK?"

"Yes. But we'd need a really isolated booth. I can't take a chance on being overheard. I don't mean to be so mysterious but... maybe you'd rather not be involved. As I think about it I guess it would be better if we got some take-out and drove back to my place in Rhode Island. Would that be OK with you? I give you my word I'm not some kind of nut who would be luring a beautiful woman into his boudoir."

"For some reason I believe you. I'd like you to know, however, I have a Tai Kwan Do Black Belt so be prepared." She said with a smile.

They packed up a few bottles of beer, then grabbed food at the nearest Chinese place and headed for Rhode Island. Once at the little house the band had used, they sat in the car and looked at each other. Then he made his decision. He wanted to see her more. If so, she needed to know a whole lot more and he needed to be the one to let her know.

He opened his door and crossed over to her side opening hers with a bow. Once in the living quarters of the home they settled their food on the coffee table and hungrily devoured every bite.

It had been a long day for each of them and Chance again tried to talk himself out of going on. She would be so much better off without his baggage he knew but his need overcame his hesitation again.

"I'm so glad you agreed to join me tonight, Jess." He began. "We've been sort of friends for nearly a year now and I'm hoping for better things. The thing is I have a problem which is momentarily ruling my life. Would you be OK with it if I just lay it out there? There probably would be some danger in the future if I follow through with what I have in mind, so please don't hesitate to call this evening to a halt right now."

"Oh, for God's sakes, Chance, stop beating around the bushes and get on with it. I give you my word I'm a big girl and I'll make my own decisions. It's always better to know what's what before any commitment." Jessie said, and then settled back to hear.

Chance told her his story just as he had to his manager and best friend, Luther Banks. Jessie reacted very much as Luther had; with sympathy and disbelief. In less than an hour he finished and silence filled the room. Then, suddenly he spoke again,

"I thought that that guitar was my salvation at the time, but now I know that was not true. It's now obvious to me that it might have been. It did make a great difference in my life but it is you who I hope will continue to be my salvation.

111

"The thing is, I have made plans to do away with my nightmares and I've already put them in the works. It's not my desire to do away with the great Gertz pair but I surely am ready to call their bluff. I was told recently that they both are thinking of furthering their political positions. Andre, it seems, feels he's ready for a senate run and Gladys says privately that she has some great plans for Branfield if they elect her as mayor. I'm involved in calling those big schemes to a halt and if I'm successful maybe I'll be able to sleep again.

"I'd like to continue seeing you but not until this mess is cleaned up. Damn. This sounds maniacal when put like that. I guess I'll just leave it at that and get you home."

"Look, Chance, I confess I'm not in any hurry to get involved in some dangerous vendetta. I have just begun to break even at JESSIE'S, I have my place in pretty good shape, and I'm not really in the mood for some big criminal activity. If you think you must do this thing I understand. I'd probably use the lawyer in me and nail them. Even though this all took place many years ago, I think there would be no statute of limitations on such a heinous crime. Why wouldn't that be a better option for you? I'd be glad to call a lawyer I know in Boston. He's fascinated with family law and child abuse and I know he'd go for this. What do you say?"

"That's a great idea, Jess, but I don't think so. I believe I need to see this through myself and I'm OK with whatever comes of my ideas. I can't imagine I could live another week without at least calling their bluff. I admit I'd rather have my hands around his throat, but just seeing him squirm would make my day."

"You know, Chance, I understand you think you're right but revenge sometimes has bad consequences. Be careful, what you wish for." Jess pleaded.

CHAPTER X

THE DEED IS IN WORKS

The rental in Rhode Island the band had lived in while on the Boston gig, was just right for his plan to take shape. As it happened the boys in the band decided not to live there and instead scattered to visit old stomping grounds. After all, they had performed in this neck of the woods off and on and had many friends to visit. Chance, on the other hand, spent the next week formulating his plan-who in the world would believe such a thing? He thought. No one, that's who. In fact, he was counting on its bizarreness to be his cover.

One day he even dreamed up a disguise, then rented a four year old Toyota sedan and went to Branfield himself just to case the town again. He felt he needed to visualize the whole thing more carefully. One didn't take on a major project like this without a lot of planning. He didn't worry about what would happen to him though he'd sure miss

Jessie if it failed. What the Hell, if it worked he might be able to sleep again. If it failed jail couldn't be any worse than his life now.

His first step was a cruise through the town. Wow. He thought to himself. I did look at some old maps from the days when I lived here but from what I see Denver would need to change his lyrics, now. The old home town surely did not look the same. There was even a shopping mall, a couple of new groceries, and a Macy's on the edge of town. When he needed some aspirin for the headache that suddenly hit him, there was Walgreens right on Orange St. And to top it all off, he'd helped a beautiful little girl get a card for her dad.

'Well, well, Chance old boy." He muttered aloud. "You're now a philanthropist."

His next stop was to look at the house. That would be the hardest thing he'd done in the last many years. Just the thought of looking at it made his nerve ends quiver. God damn! What was the matter with him? It was 2022 for God's sakes. He was now 50 years old. Wouldn't it be logical that anyone could move on at this age? Especially a person who had been as successful as he had?

"We'll see." He announced to his windshield. "Am I up to this? Will it make anything better? Will this revengeful thing he had planned soothe his angst? Maybe I should see a shrink first. No way. I'll take a look and then have a major man to man with Luther. He'd give good advice."

With that thought it was at least settled in his mind. One of the richest men in the musical world, Morris George Chance vowed to embark on what easily could really be his last performance. He pulled down his hat, buttoned up his long black coat and started the car.

"Would his 'mother' even recognize him if she saw him in town?" He asked himself aloud. His detective had said she might have some idea of who he was, but it was hard to believe. It had been a good 30+ years since their last encounter. Once more the big question: Why had she stayed? There was no way he could imagine what the place looked like now.

"Enough of this meandering, Chance muttered... Where would Branfield's wondrous mayor be at 10AM on May 8, 2022? He's the one of interest here."

He'd done a lot of research in the past months. Even gone to Google Search and found they showed views taken by drones of any address in the state, probably the world. He set it up and was amazed. His impression was that things had changed immensely. There were houses everywhere and even an apartment tower. In spite of what Google showed, maybe the house was gone. OK. Calm down. There's a sign for Rollins' RIVER VIEW ESTATES. Big gated community it says. He wondered why the town needed gates. He pulled the car over and began to laugh. As it had been for the past year or so the tears took over and he allowed himself to weep.

"Get hold of yourself, man. You knew this wouldn't be easy. The question is will it matter? Will you be whole for the first time in your life? What is it they say now? Put on your 'big boy pants' and act or bury it."

Why in the hell would he know what was what here? What did he expect? He'd only seen the outside of the place for a couple of days when he was 10 years old and then again one October night after he turned 14! God! That's 50 years ago; a life time for some. Was that true? Why does it feel like yesterday every day?

Just past the Rollin's compound, there is was. Standing exactly where Google said it was. The home he didn't really know at all from so many years ago. His mother had told him that this was where his great grandparents, Gustave and Maude had first lived and where neighbors had helped Andre Jan grow up.

"OK, Chance, if that one was the site of his nightmares, let's see who's living in old Gus's place now."

With that thought, he parked the Toyota in a front yard; made sure his hat, coat, and dark glasses were in place and ambled up to knock on the cottage door.

It was an unbelievable feeling. Here he was knocking on the door of a place he had lived in for 4 years! And yet, he had no idea of what it had looked like. This was certainly a fool's errand. The door eked open and then was immediately slammed.

"Wait. Wait. I just have a question. I didn't mean to startle you." He said as he knocked again. "Please give me a minute to explain. I was just interested for a friend. He said it might be something he would like to know more about if I was ever in town. You know, like how the place looked now. And, as far as the location goes, I, myself might be interested in buying the house if you wish to discuss it."

The door opened an inch or so and she appeared once more. She carried a small child of maybe a year or so. He was not happy and squalled letting everyone in the vicinity know. He estimated she was about 30 or so and appeared very pretty underneath her tough demeanor. If one could ignore the tired look in her brown eyes and the sagging way she held herself, she would light up a room. Obviously, her life had bottomed out and she had no idea what to do next.

"Why in the world would anyone want this dump?" She grumbled over the child's cries. "It hasn't seen any care for the whole two years I've been here. Are you kidding me?"

"Please let me explain." Chance said gently. "I used to have a friend who lived here years ago and I just need a small place for a while. I've been looking for something local but livable and this looks solid. I'm pretty handy so I'm sure I could fix it up. Do you live here alone?"

"Not really. I am divorced but I've got a little girl in school plus Henry here. My friend Dave comes around regularly. He's due just now so I'd recommend you move along and maybe find a real estate office to help you." Mary Riley said through the crack in the door. Then he heard the click of a deadbolt.

"I tell you what. I'll leave a slip of paper here with my offer and you can talk to your man as to what you want to do. I'm on the road so I'll have someone contact you in a few days to see if it is anything you want to do. Have a nice day." He turned and walked down the driveway he could not remember.

Chance drove the Toyota past to the great manor down the street. Within a quarter mile or so there it stood; regal, impressive, and stately. Was this the trade-off that he had offered good old Gladys?

The huge brick edifice sat up on a knoll, the better to oversee the town, he surmised. He estimated it to have 3-5 acres of manicured grounds around the perimeters. And, of course it could only be entered through the ever present gate and long driveway. As he got closer there was the expected sign: black shiny background and gold letters announcing that this was GERTZ MANOR. Another stood nearby: ADAM'S INC. SECURITY painted boldly near the gate.

This was where the town's wondrous, respected, most successful mayor lived: This was Andre Jan Gertz' and his wife Gladys' domain. This was where Chance hoped to pull off the coup that would appease his hate and salve his soul.

He drove by and continued a bit on his recon mission. Though growing in population he could see that somehow Branfield had managed to retain most of its small town/city reputation. The shops on Main St. presented themselves with clean, swept sidewalks, and the gas stations were obviously required to do the same. Betty's Coffee Shoppe was entered through a slate walkway festooned with bright flowers and even the diner at the end near the library was newly painted and signed: HERM'S. He guessed correctly that there were no manufacturing or large offices allowed. With the exception of Rollins Inc. found near the edge of Ash St. he saw none. Must be because of their place when the town was beginning, he thought. There were, of course, an occasional dentist or doctor with welcoming entrances, and the ever present real estate and insurance sales offices facing the street.

"I'd say this berg is under lock and key to somebody." He said to no one. "From my investigator, I bet I know."

It wasn't difficult to get an ear full in this small blue collar town. As Chance wandered through Branfield-a breakfast here, and dinner there, Herm's Bar once in a while, the main topic often was their town mayor. No one was above discussing the many idiosyncrasies of the town's GENIUS SAVANTE, Andre Jan Gertz. Tales were told of his

117

having an engineering degree from Dartmouth or UNH. It was said that over the years while they were keeping track of Old Pap he had been getting his education. Some discussed it with his teachers at BHS and were filled in about the particulars. Yes he had gone to college. And yes, he had always been a quiet but brilliant scholar. Mr. Ravineau, the principal at BHS did mention that Andre was quite manipulative. He had seen it in the way Andre had been able to get the votes needed to be in the Honor Society and again when though tied with Gene McGuire in grades, he had influenced the school board to elect him. The year before he graduated from college the man had been offered any job he wanted at the local General Electric plant in Massachusetts. Some believed that at one time he had had the ear of Washington itself and that NASA was where it was today in great part due to the early contributions of one Andre Jan Gertz.

All agreed that he was the luckiest thing that ever happened to Branfield. There were a few who mentioned that they wondered if the town had given away too much power to him, especially because his wife was also their employee.

They were unsure about his wife, Gladys. She was an excellent town clerk that was for sure but she certainly wasn't anything else. One could hardly remember ever seeing her smile. Even when nominated for the town's "Most honorable citizen" in 1992 she had said no more than a quiet thank you.

Many in town discussed the odd marriage over afternoon shopping and it always came up at HERMS after four. Why in the world had he chosen her? For that matter why would she have chosen to marry him at all? There were some men who considered themselves friends of Andre but those few had no answer. They were an unusual couple that was for sure. Some used stronger language such as weird or peculiar but all agreed as long as they were not asking them, they'd move on.

The thing was that Andre had always been in town. He had always been a clever business man and had perfected his social graces to a tee. He knew when to ask about a new baby, how to say, "Merry Christmas" to everyone he met. It didn't hurt his reputation that he always opened doors for women, asked how their family was getting along or expressed his support for anyone affected by a loss in the family. It wasn't that the town's people really trusted him but you had to give the man credit. He had made himself the best the town had to offer.

The town was flourishing and there were upwards of 20,200 residents now living in Branfield. The town's founders felt that it would soon become necessary to limit the type of people who might want to live their chosen way of life. They had been looking for someone who might be able to lead them away from the influx of undesirables and felt they had found it. Andre Gertz had been in town for many years. He had established a good rapport with the townspeople and his hardware store was a great addition to the community. His presentations at their town meetings had always been understandable, well-researched, and almost always successful. By **1992, t**he movers and shakers saw him as their problem solver extraordinaire.

After many phone calls and over morning coffee Abe Hindale, their town manager was elected to approach Andre with a proposition. It took no time at all. Andre was ready. He had always seen himself as an organizer and was ripe for flattery. He had positioned himself for just such a day. With Gladys help he had carte blanche to the wishes of the backroom politicians.

"Andre thanks for meeting me." Abe said offering his hand. "Have a seat and let's order. I'm a big fan of Betty's Apple Fritters. Ever tried them?"

"Wouldn't get through the morning without one." Andre Jan replied. "Whenever I need a big pick-up I come here, you know. They've got the best coffee in town too."

It was amazing. Abe had been sent to find his friends a suitable candidate for the office of Mayor. It needed to be someone who would approve of having such a position and he needed to have a resounding enthusiasm before even being asked. Abe had even written down his talking points and rehearsed his spiel before offering it to Andre. Almost before he could get his offer out on the table, Abe had his answer.

"Yes. I'm very flattered." Said Andre, and then he took charge. "Will this election be soon? Let's see. It's now January. I'd imagine you'd want to advertise for other candidates. Am I to understand that you and some others would be voting in my favor? And, would I need to campaign much? I've a store to run you know. And, not that it matters, but does this position come with a salary?"

Within only two town meetings he soon managed to engineer a solution for their population fears by getting laws passed limiting the types of businesses that could be opened and most of all by requiring all independent home builders as well as Rollins Inc. to build homes with no less than five acres of land. Only the crème de la crème would be welcome in Branfield, he would say.

The old guard ate it up. His propositions were enthusiastically followed, and the result was often sad. It seemed that more and more children born and raised in Branfield and just starting out found themselves unable to stay in their own neighborhoods. Everything was too expensive. Chance found some people who even talked of replacing their town manager who was anxious to solve the problems and was constantly proposing that the town allow Rollins to build the 10 3- story apartments on the edge of town to help some stay. These people were working quietly to find a candidate who could win the next election. If successful, most of the average person's salary would leave no chance for a home. Chance was sure he knew which side of the issues his nemesis would take.

It looked to Chance as if Andre knew there were a few naysayers but saw no reason to offer to change the town's policies. In addition, he was more and surer that there had to have been some kind of agreement he and Gladys had made. To the townspeople, the couple was happy, popular, and successful. It looked like all was going well.

"Well, Father let's see what you say when you see just what you raised. I can't wait to let you know what I can do." With that, he drove toward Jessie's and a few beers.

CHAPTER XI

RECRIMINATION

"So mother," He sneered. "How have you been? Any trouble around here I should know about? Leading the good life with the father of the year?" Gladys blanched at his bitter tone. "Oh, come now. You must have had some idea about who could have upset your apple cart. I do understand though. You two have been without equal for years; practically no faults, I hear."

"Please, Paul. Must you be so cruel? Have you forgotten it was I who saved you? "Give it a rest, mother. Take a good long look at the last 36 years of your life. Thirty six years. Now that's a bit of a stretch to believe that you had done no wrong. I'll bet even the most successful of all popes would not be able to make such a claim."

Gladys' countenance looked grayer by the minute but she made one last try. "Paul, why would you think this has been a bed of roses for me? Look at me. I must look nearly 90 years old compared to most folks. I retired last year you know. They gave me a gold watch and a party. Whoopee."

"And what did Andre do, might I ask?" grumbled Paul. Then he snapped his fingers. "I'll bet I know. He gave a speech announcing his most recent successes, right? How did he connect your celebrations to it? Did he say how much help you have been? Did he list the many times you supplied him with insider information? Did he say 'The love of my life has made it all worth it for us?' Or..."

"Stop it. Stop it. I can't go on this way." His 'mother' screamed. "You're right. He's a monster. He's the most narcissistic man the world has ever seen. So what? I got you out of it. I sent you away for an education. I didn't even try to find you when you headed out from HARROW. I...should never have been born, I guess." Her anguish filled the room. Chance almost caved. Jessie's words filled his brain.

'Chance my love. There will be no future for us if you go on with your plans.' Jessie's words echoed in his brain. He hesitated just long enough for Mayor Andre Jan Gertz to enter the room.

"I'll be dammed, if it isn't the wandering son. Where the hell have you been all this time? And, may I ask, why now? If you're looking for money just forget it. I washed that possibility from my mind many years ago." Andre's voice dripped with scorn. "Gladys, why didn't you call me so I could be prepared? I probably wouldn't have sent Bill off with the car."

He turned once more giving Paul a chance to see him more closely. It was amazing. He still had a full head of hair; black straight hair. His stature seemed smaller than he remembered. Was he really always less than six feet tall? Did he always have that paunch and wear those tinted glasses? How could this guy he was looking at have been able to put such fear in him? And Gladys? She was still dressed in what looked like quality goods but that certainly didn't enhance her demeanor. The blond styled locks he remembered had turned gray and been put into a bun. Wrinkles had overtaken her makeup. He wondered if he would even have recognized her on a crowded street. He wondered if she would be able to survive what he had planned for his 'long-ago-parents'...

"Gladys, how in the world did this vagabond get into our home? Did you plan this? If not, why did you let him in? Have you lost your mind?"

"I don't know, Andre." Gladys murmured. "I heard a knock on the door and just assumed it would be your driver or a delivery or...I don't know. But he's here. My boy is here." She crumpled into the rocker behind her.

"Well I know what to say. I'll tell you just once, Paul." Father began. "This is my home. GERTZ MANOR. I don't want to have you here. I have no interest in kumbaya. I did the best I could for you and would have given you wonderful opportunities in life. You threw it into the sewer you have been living in I assume and I will not forgive you for that. Look at Mother. Have you made her happy? Does she look like the success she should have been? Not on your life. She's spent over 30 years hoping you would call, or write, or look us up. Hah! You have destroyed her."

"By God, Father, I give you this. You haven't changed a bit. Still the same smug, self-centered bully I remember." sneered Chance. "I imagine you really have convinced yourself that you were the best thing ever to happen to my Aunt Gladys or to me. What a buffoon you are!"

He caught himself getting too angry and then calmly added: "Seeing as I'm in charge here, why don't you have a seat next to your beloved and we'll get on with the next part of your lives."

"You've got to be kidding, Paul." Andre shouted. "You're in charge now? Do you know who I am? I've got friends in very high places and you're going to regret this." He said as he retrieved his iPhone from his pocket.

"Oops, my man, that's not going to be." Chance said as he grabbed it and threw it into the bag he carried.

123

"OK, Mother, let's have yours as well. No crying now." Gladys did as ordered and sat back down.

"Remember how you used to come into my cage and pronounce what I was to do each hour of each day? Guess what? I'm giving the orders now. So, this is how the next few days or months of you lives are going to go. I haven't decided how long this will last yet as it depends on how you handle the whole thing. And don't be looking around. I've had all of the security bells and whistles you have put into this edifice disabled. This is just for us. The three happiest family members I know."

With that he pulled two sets of handcuffs from the pockets of the black coat he wore, grabbed Andre's arms and twisted them to attach the cuffs at his back. Gladys hadn't moved. He didn't even have to ask. She now just turned in her chair and offered her bony wrists to him. Who would have believed the vision even if they saw it?

"Do you think this has all been peaches and cream for me? And now, look what you have done." Gladys said in one last try.

"That's of no concern to me, Mother. You and dear old Father are all that matters at this point in my life." He answered. "There is really nothing I can think of that could possibly atone for what you've done. I have no sympathy for either of you. Now, let's get on with it."

It was midnight in Branfield, NH. Clouds announcing the arrival of a big rain storm had covered any light which might illuminate the three people who trod slowly through the adjoining forests. Andre had bought all five acres between the two homes making it was easy to go unnoticed. Within minutes they entered the back door of their first home and he shepherded them down to the wine cellar.

"For God's Sakes, Paul, what in hell are you doing? It's cold down here and your Mother hasn't been well and..." Andre began to whine. "Stop this foolishness right now and let's call this fiasco a draw."

"Wow. Now that's a good idea. I wonder why I didn't think to ask the same of you so many years ago. Now, let's see, if I've calculated correctly, there's a screw here under the last stair. Ah ha! Look what I've found." He exclaimed as a six foot section of the wine shelf twisted and then stopped in a position perpendicular to itself.

"I'll be dammed. If it isn't the coziest home for a 10 year old I have ever seen. I always wondered how it would appeal to someone of your age. And look. It's been refurbished. There's the same old bed but I do see new bedding and there's the bathroom with the leaky shower. There are a mess of books on the table under the one light. Let's see...OPEN SESAME." He shouted as Mother grew smaller and smaller in her stance. The cage door opened wide on his command.

"Now Father let's see how you are suited to a new life; a life of knowledge, of introspection, of hopelessness, penance and frustration. Rise, old man, and enter. This is to be your home for some time and Mother. You will be the ever present jailer. I wouldn't think you'd need any preparation as you've been here before, remember? No? Well, drag out the memories you two. This isn't over until I say it is."

With that, he clutched Andre's arm tightly and placed him in the little chair near the bed, then unlocked his handcuffs. Next, he stepped outside the bars locking the heavy metal door behind him and then directed Gladys to sit in a chair which he had placed just to the right near a small desk.

"OK, everybody? Here are the rules of our little game." Chance said as he passed out a folder to each of his captives. "As you see, there is a set for each of you. Each of you has different goals here and I'm expecting them to be followed. I don't think this should take two years but we'll see."

FATHER GERTZ SUPPLIES

3 shirts	3 trousers
2 sets of underwear	1 sweatshirt
1 jacket	2 sheet sets
2 towels	1 wash cloth
3 pairs of socks	1 pair of shoes
1 night robe	2 pair pajamas
Soap, tooth paste	1 brush and 1 comb

FATHER GERTZ RULES

"The rules will be familiar to you, Andre, as I have used those under which I lived for TWO LONG YEARS. Remember?"

"As you see there are 3 articles and 3 books piled on the table. You are to read at least one each day and then compose an essay about them. Then be prepared to discuss them from 6AM TO 9AM TWO DAYS LATER. A satisfactory response to my questions will shorten your stay by one week."

MOTHER GERTZ SUPPLIES

3 dresses 2 pair of slacks	3 sweaters
1 warm jacket	3 sets of underwear
1 pair shoes	4 pair socks
3 night gowns	1 pair slippers
Towels, soap, shampoo	Brush, comb

MOTHER GERTZ RULES

"You will be living above in the home you so dearly loved. I have seen to it that you will have a fully stocked kitchen.

Mother, you will have exactly the same rules as so long ago. Namely:

1.   You will be responsible for any laundry your beloved may need done.

2.   You will be making 3 meals a day, each with enough food for two.

3.   You will bring those 3 meals each day to dear old "dad" always at the same time. His meals and other needs will need to be given to him through the bars as you will not have a key. You will sit outside in your chair and join him.

Breakfast menu: oatmeal, milk, and an orange. To be served at 9am each day

Lunch menu: Peanut butter and jelly sandwich made with whole wheat bread, milk and an apple. To be served at 12:30pm

Dinner menu: Baked beans, cooked cabbage, 1 chicken leg, 2 chocolate cookies. To be served at 6: PM

THERE IS TO BE NO VARIATION TO THIS MENU FOR THE LENGTH OF YOUR STAY."

FINALLY, WE WILL ALL DECIDE HOW THIS WILL END. THAT WILL BE EXPLAINED TO YOU AFTER 14 DAYS TOGETHER.

"There. Is that all clear? Any questions?" No one moved. "By the way, there is a copy in your GREEN folder of the memo you have sent to the town hall explaining your absence. As of now, you are gone

127

for a month of reflection and rest. The timing will change with the level of cooperation you show as we go.

"OK Andre, now that you're in your luxury apartment let's get rid of those cuffs. Just back up a bit and I'll unlock them. When you have a minute, look over the articles and books you see on your little desk. The list is in no particular order. You'll be surprised at how much better you'll feel after you've read them. And I wouldn't be surprised if your lovely wife might enjoy them as well."

The reading materials were:

1. Why We Stay: A Deeper Look at Domestic Abuse
06/06/2016 05:36 pm ET **Updated** Dec 06, 2017   HUFFF POST ALI

2. 10 Ways to Let Go of the Need to Control
Often times, the path we so desperately want to be on is not the most valuable or productive one. Letting go of control means more   joy, freedom, peace, connection and support. So here are 10 ways to let go of control and embrace the art of surrender.
By Lauren Stahl, contributor

3. Emotionally Abusive Men and Women: Who Are They?
By Natasha Tracy

4. Walking On Eggshells
by Jane Issey

5. Taking Sides
by David M. Hall

6. Compassionate Child Rearing
by Robert W. Firestone, PHD

"Gladys will be copying down the order in which you wish to study them and give it to me when I arrive for our discussion and evaluation. We will begin the day after tomorrow at exactly 6AM." He remarked as he checked the lock on the cage and then left.

The two of them had not moved nor spoken. He wondered if that would be how it would go. He checked his iPhone for the time. It was time to get some rest to be in shape for the next visit.

CHAPTER XII

CHOICES

He'd studied and researched for months trying to find the safest way one could obtain a weapon. Yes, he had to admit that was his goal- a lethal weapon-a piece of metal which would soothe all of his angst away. It struck him as odd that with all of his experience on the road he had no idea how it was done. He'd surely read enough detective stories whose protagonist could have one in a few minutes. He'd tried the dark streets of Boston but found his courage lacking. How in the world did anyone know who had a gun or who might be ready to use it for your wallet or your life for that matter? Finally, in need to get his plan moving, he took the big chance. The simplicity of modern crime astounded him.

He'd gone out for a drive and stopped in at a small gun shop he'd seen once before. Sure enough, he had found it to be just what he wanted. In the little out-of-the-way corner store near the Rhode Island border no one seemed surprised at his request at all. In fact they hadn't even taken the time to ask for his credentials after he found what he wanted. Within a short time, the owner had shown him three suitable hand guns. Chance told him that it would be used only for his own protection and the owner suggested a few lessons he gave on Saturdays but didn't insist. The weapon now sat on the table before him and waited for his next move.

A week ago he had bought a small cage in an out-of-the-way corner hardware store near Providence. He had taken great care to choose a regular old cage. It was obviously just right for a small cat or other animal any parent would be looking for. The cage was dull, cheap galvanized metal with a small door that could be easily locked from the back. Nothing fancy for the task planned; nothing that could be traced easily just in case. There was some doubt in his mind as to whether or not he should worry about it being traced. He was too focused on what it was for. The mission had taken over his consciousness. Sleep had become impossible but he didn't care. The mirror didn't care either, throwing back clear visions of the deep furrows he had acquired in the last four months. He placed the gun in the cage and made sure the lock was secure.

Two days later, with his great plan in place, Chance was ready to go back for his next encounter with his captives. This would be the routine for the foreseeable future. The last thing would be to offer a solution. It was up the two of them now. There was no way to predict how they would react to the choice he had in mind. Either it would work or he'd have to let him go and disappear quickly himself.

Early on June 22, 2022 he put on his disguise and headed for Branfield. He assumed that at this early hour no one would be out to see him but chose not to make it easy. He let himself in and headed straight for the wine cellar wondering all the way what he would see.

There they were; Gladys asleep in her lounge chair just outside the cage and Andre sitting in his old chair tapping his foot while trying to write.

"Well, well. Look who's here. Andre sneered. "At least you learned something from me. Being on time was my first lesson, remember?" He went on.

"Oh, I remember old man; all too well. But let's not quibble about a few years of my life. What have you got for me? Which thought have you read and where is your report?" Chance said struggling to keep his voice quiet but forceful.

"You've got to be kidding. Did you really think I would do as you asked? See that list and the books? Do they look touched to you?" Father answered. "You're even more stupid than I thought."

At this point Gladys rose from her night's rest and headed for the kitchen. Chance thought probably to make breakfast.

"I tell you what, Andre; I'll give you a reprieve: 15 minutes to read and write some reaction to the first article; do it now or there will be no food today. It's now 6:30. I'll return at 6:45." With that he left the room.

When he returned he was carrying a box about 4 feet square and stopped to invite Gladys to accompany him.

"You'll need to be present for this Mother." He said. "You can get your breakfast fast enough after this is done." She followed him to the secret room without a sound.

"OK, Dad. Let's see what you've done and then we'll open the box."

Andre handed him a piece of paper with one sentence at the top. It read:

Paul Richard Medford Gertz is a criminal and should be immediately arrested.

"Wonderful to see you know when you're in real trouble, Andre. I didn't want to do this but let's finish your options." Chance said as he opened the box and placed its contents on Gladys' desk/table.

There before their eyes stood a box about one foot on all sides. It appeared to be made of some kind of steel bars and had a small but

133

strong looking lock on a side door. Inside laid a Colt 45, shined and menacing. Next to it were two keys.

"So, Gladys, as you see your beloved has decided not to cooperate, at least for today. As a result, you will be in control from now on so listen carefully. The gun over there is loaded with one bullet. It is up to you if it ever gets used. There are two keys there as well. The largest one is for this room and it will allow you to leave and padlock this room from the outside. The smaller key is for this cage and will allow you three options.

#1: Free the man of your dreams and flee

#2: Go to the authorities.

#3: You can just use the bullet on Branfield's mayor and then leave alone and free. Of course, there's always the possibility that your hubby will behave and produce some interesting reading for me. That will solve the whole dilemma. We'll see.

"Also, I want you both to have this red folder which contains copies of all of the drawings I made during my time with the two of you, the actual tickets I used as a 14 year old when I went to Laramie, Wyoming, as well as records from HARROW MILITARY ACADEMY and records identifying me from the US ARMY. I believe all of which would put you both in jeopardy if I turned them in to your local police.

"I am going to leave now and hope to see you again when I return in two days. Mother, maybe you can persuade him to produce a more appropriate essay then. Or...who knows?" The door closed quietly behind him.

An hour passed as he made his way back to Rhode Island. The nearer he got the more confused he became. What the hell, he told himself. I had to do something and this just puts the whole thing in their court...well in her court, I guess...of course he's a great talker and has convinced her before...maybe they'll just get him out and I'll never see either of them again. I had to do something. Had to??? I don't know if I should have done that. What if it doesn't make a difference? Maybe this is not the way to go. His brain began to swirl in all directions.

"God Dammit! Have I lost my nerve?" He said out loud. "I'm a grown man. I've tons of cash, I have fame, and I'm really OK. Did I need to pull this off? Is it too late to undo? I've met a woman who might be willing to share some of what's left. Maybe what I need is a friend-a confidante. And just maybe it should be her."

With that, he picked up his I-phone and dialed without having the slightest idea of what to say.

Jessie answered on the first ring. "Listen Jess, it's me. Is there any way I could meet with you and talk? I've got some real problems here and...Aw, Hell, Jessie, this is just a shot in the dark. You don't owe me anything, I know. I'll just hang up now."

He was the luckiest man in the world as it happened, though later he would consider the great Andre Jan Gertz better eligible to take that title.

"Hi, Chance." She said brightly. "Don't you dare hang up. What are you talking about? Where are you? I'm at the bar tonight and it's ah, let me see quarter to one. I'm buried under boredom. Why don't you drop in now and we'll have a chance to shoot the breeze. I'll be closing in a few minutes; it's been a slow night. It's a Wednesday so I'm off until noon tomorrow. "

"I don't know what's got into me." Chance answered. "I forgot you were still open. Sorry, you must be exhausted. Let's just let this go. I'll give you a call another day."

"No you don't my friend. Look, I'm here. I'm not tired and I can tell when a situation is important. Get in that fancy car you have and I'll see you at the back door. I'm locking up the front right now. The beer is cold and if you're hungry there's plenty of food in the fridge. Move!" and Jessie hung up.

Well, well, well. She thought in the next few minutes. All this time of arm's length relations and Bang! He needs my counsel. Hmmm.

135

He's always been polite and mysterious so...probably just had a spat with a girl friend or wife or who knows. OK, Jessie run a comb through, add a bit of color to your face, and let's play Dr. Phil.

An hour later, she heard the light knock on the back door. Cautiously, she lifted the peep hole cover she had had installed and then hit the security code on the wall.

"Hi there Chance." She said brightly as she let him in. "Kind of cold out there. Maybe we should head upstairs to my place and light the fireplace if that's not too forward of me."

"That sounds good, thanks. This will take a while though so please tell me right now that you promise to throw me out at the first inkling that I should not continue."

"Agreed. I can't imagine what the matter is but I do know how good it is to have someone to listen. I'm good at that. Someday I'll regale you with tales of my life with mom." She laughed.

He relaxed but refused to remove his hat or his long black coat. She chose not to insist and they headed upstairs.

As the lights lit up her living area he was stunned. He had always expected that she was a woman struggling to make ends meet living above her little bar hoping to climb out of debt someday. This was not what lay before him. The furniture was not that which he'd seen at the great Manor. This was new and modern. Bright and cheery and the view over the lake across the street was amazing. Breathtaking in the night's full moon, actually.

"Have a seat anywhere." Jessie said. "I'll get the fire going and maybe you'll decide to take off that damn coat-perhaps the hat as well. What is that about anyway? Are you in disguise? Do I know you? Have I managed to put myself in some kind of grave danger?"

My God! I hadn't even thought. She pronounced to herself. Well what's done is done.

"How about a beer?" She offered.

As he accepted he a spied the leather lounger nearest the windows and took a seat, removing neither the coat nor the hat. He knew he'd have to but it had been so long his courage was gone. Could be it would ruin this friendship they'd established...or she'd feel she needed to kick his butt out...perhaps, he was just a coward! Get on with it, Chance. He placed the coat and hat on one of the hooks near the door and returned to his perch, naked of his cover.

Jessie returned from her kitchen, a beer in each hand and took the seat opposite his.

"Well now." She observed. "You've certainly surprised me. I've been expecting some old duffer with wrinkles and no teeth. That was obviously wrong. What I'm seeing is a rather handsome guy of fairly young age who it appears has all of his ivories and more. That damn coat didn't do justice to your height either. I had no idea you were well over six feet. And blond hair??? What in the world? If I were on the stand, I'd swear you had black hair." She leaned over and grabbed the hat and Lo! The answer was clear. "Geez. You've pasted black locks inside the brim. OK. Let's have it. You must be on the lam from something."

"No, not really." He broke in. "I think I'm on the run toward something. I haven't thought about anything else for what seems like a life time. I'm not sure anymore." His hand shook as he took the offered beer. "I fell apart today and didn't know where to turn. Bad luck for you, I guess. I couldn't think of anyone who could help. I'll go right now. Sorry." Chance said as he rose to get his things.

"You have got to be kidding. You think you could get me to bring you up here, get you a beer and a warm place to rest and then let you go out that door. You are crazier than you appear! Get on with it. First of all, is Chance your real name and if not, what is it? That shouldn't be too hard. Where are you from? Do you work for a living? Who in the world are you?"

"As you know my real name is Paul Richard Middleton. At one time my last name became Gertz. I now go under the name, Morris George Chance. I have lived and worked all over the world but currently I'm ensconced in a small house over the border in Rhode Island. In the meantime, I have bought a small home in Branfield and that's a whole other story. I am not employed at this time and I'd doubt that I ever will try the world again." At that, he fell back in the chair and closed his eyes.

For a minute she thought he might have passed away but then noticed that his chest was moving. She went to the couch, returned with her mother's last effort at crocheting, and placed it carefully over the tall exhausted stranger in her home.

Hours later, his eyes and ears snapped to attention. He couldn't see any bars. There weren't any books near his bed. That nightmare man wasn't at his door. But, where was he? What in the world had he done now and who was rattling metal in some other part of the house? Metal. That's what had awakened him! How come he couldn't see the keys? He could hear them. Panic took over his senses. He thought he should yell. There might be a chance Gladys would come in. Breathing came only in gulps. Sweat invaded his t-shirt. Ten minutes went by and the ogre didn't appear. Slowly he pulled the cover down and tried to calm himself.

"Is anyone here? Hello?" he spoke into the room. "What's going on? And where the hell am I?"

He looked around again and again but couldn't remember anything about the last few hours. In fact he couldn't seem to tell if it was night or day. Within a minute, Jessie was by his side.

"Hey. Hey. I'd say you've had a nightmare. Here, have a sip. It's just hot coffee but it might help you get your bearings. I'm so sorry. I shouldn't have made such a clatter in the kitchen. You were sleeping so soundly. I tried but..."

"Jessie? Jessie? Oh my God. Jessie! What have I done? I'm so sorry I didn't mean to alarm you. I guess these nightmares of mine will never go away." He uttered as he sat up. "What time is it? I think I might have an appointment today. What day is it?"

"Look, my friend. Relax. It's Sunday and only 7am. We have all day to straighten this out. Why don't you hit the shower. There's one right down that hall and I've put in new towels and stuff. Give it a try and perhaps it'll shake whatever it is that gets these things going. Meanwhile I'll whip up some scrambled eggs and a pound or two of bacon. You do like bacon, I hope?"

A half hour later, the curtains had been opened and the east was announcing the arrival of the day. Great long golden lights emblazoned the way for the sun. A different man immerged from the hall.

"Well. That was embarrassing. Some way to introduce yourself to a new woman in your life! Again, I want to apologize. You were kind enough to welcome me into this beautiful home and I went into hysterics." She watched as he wrestled with his breath. "Whew! I think I'm getting dizzy would you mind if we sat down somewhere?" He said.

"Of course. C'mon let's sit over here near the window. You need something to eat. I'll get our breakfast and bring it here. I'll bet that will put some life into you. Can I help you move? Here. Take my arm and let's give it a try. "

With her encouragement, Chance made the window seat. Within 10 minutes he felt his mind clear. Jessie arrived with a TV tray and a breakfast feast. The bacon was crispy, there were two eggs sunny side up, and she had even made muffins.

"This is above and beyond, you know." He said as Jessie sat beside him with her own loaded plate. "I don't think I've had a better meal in any of the high class restaurants I've been to; Paris can't hold a candle. Does this mean we might learn to like each other?"

A comfortable quiet fell over them as they ate and enjoyed the glorious view. Finally, Jessie made the first move.

"I would hope we could make a stab at it-the friendship. I would love to have a person to gab and gallivant with. You know, I still only know what you want me to call you. Chance, is that right? You never told me what drove you here or what is practically killing you."

"I don't know how now." He said. "I'm afraid that my problems might destroy us. They're pretty serious. That is, if I even get out of the mess I'm in. Could we just spend a little more time here alone, without

139

the world butting in? I'd like to pretend we can be happy and safe and maybe more."

"Paul, Chance, or Morris, whoever you are, I say let's give it a go. How about just for today? Then we'll see if we like each other enough to go on. I'll clear these dishes away and you can do whatever, then we'll walk around the grounds a bit. The lake breezes will help blow the world away. "

"I'm very fond of you, Jess." He began. "If only I'd met you sooner I think we could make a go of our lives together. But, there are things going on here that you can't imagine. For now at least, I guess I'd like you to call me Morris. Also, if it's OK with you I say we just pretend to be long- time friends and not waste one more second on the outside world."

"You're on." Jessie said with a smile. Then she made a call to her cook saying she needed him to cover for a couple of days. With that and almost in unison as all romantics long for, they announced to each other that this had gotten to be a thing not to be dismissed.

There was no need for rules it turned out. They were both in need of a trusted place to be emotionally. They had found it. Morris held her in his arms for hours it seemed. She couldn't believe how wonderful it was to let herself just be loved. Neither questioned the length of time it would last; neither asked for endless commitment. Time was not an issue for at least 48 hours and for the time being that was enough.

He loved the massages that she offered and basked in her touch. She held her breath every time he caressed her body wishing it would never stop.

"I think I could get used to this. Thank you for being so caring and loving." Jessie murmured in his ear. "It's been a long time and..." her voice faded as she felt his touch again.

Time got away from them again and suddenly for the second time, the clock was welcoming the sun's rays into the bedroom. Morris mind shot into action.

"Jessie, its Thursday. Did you know that? How in the world could we have missed whatever the world has been doing?" he said with laughter. "You've done what I haven't been able to do for most of my life. No forward thinking; no backward nerves. I've not been this happy for so long. Music always could do it but this? This is a whole other thing. Oh, God, Jess. If I weren't in such a mess I'd say let's make a run at happiness but I'm afraid I must let the goblins in. He clutched her harder than ever then released his grip.

"It's time to face my music, Jess, so here goes."

The tale began just as it had when he told Luther after the last rehearsal. When he reached his 14th birthday he stopped and heaved a sigh.

"So that's the past but I'd better leave while I'm ahead."

"Morris." Jessie stepped in to say. "You can't expect to tell me this stuff and then run away. So, it all happened. So, what went on since you were 14? Who in the world are you now? For God's sakes, give me a break, here. Is this what you do? Make promises, offer love, a new life, and then stomp on it?"

"It's more serious than that, Jess. I've set something in motion that I can't undo; something that will probably put me right where I spent my young years and I don't know how to get out of it. In fact, I didn't think I wanted to until the last few days with you. For the first time in my life, I feel I have someone besides Luther whom I can care for and now..." He threw up his hands in complete despair.

"OK, then. I say let's call this Luther guy and get him over here. I'll bet between the three of us we can at least see some daylight for you."

"You're right, Jess. I'll give him a call and maybe he can come today."

BEVERLY A. MASSEY

142

CHAPTER XIII

LUTHER, CHANCE, & JESSIE

The call made, Jessie and Chance took time to gather their forces. Chance knew this would be a long day and wondered if he was up to it, then asked himself just how much of his situation he should foist on his best friends in the world. Was it OK to involve a friend or lover to the point that they could be liable or charged as an assessor to one's crime? Should he order the two of them to disappear when Luther arrived? Would Luther go? Should he tell them how he thought he could finish this thing he had done? Wouldn't that put them in even further jeopardy if he got charged? He had no answers.

The buzzing of the doorbell nearly sent him into hysterics again. "Pull 'em up, old man." He cautioned himself. "It's time to grow up."

There before her stood one of the handsomest men she had ever seen. He was dressed in blue jeans and a soft plaid shirt. A pair of white bottomed Sketchers topped the look off. The goatee was immaculately trimmed and he kept his graying locks carefully cut short. She felt she was looking straight into the eyes of a man who could be trusted and compassionate. He was not anywhere near the height of Chance; probably not six feet, but he stood proud making him seem even taller, somehow. His manner exuded kindness; quiet and comfortable.

"Hi, Luther," she stammered. "Come right in. I guess you already know my name but I'm Jessie Gilmore. I've somehow become very fond of your friend Paul, Morris, or Chance here. Please come in and help yourself to coffee and there are muffins nearby."

"It a pleasure." Luther said as he extended his hand. "My man here needs a lot of help I think and maybe it might have to be from the two of us. Let us hope he's still savable."

Again, the gentleness, the positive attitude, left Jessie nearly speechless. Chance hadn't said a word during the whole meeting but now rose and clutched his friend to his chest. "

"What can I say, Luth? Thanks are never enough for this kind of thing. How are you and the boys doing? How's the last album selling? Will they ever speak to me again? Oh, God. What have I done?" he nearly fell from Luther's arms. Luther turned him so that he could look straight into his eyes.

"I owe you more than ever could be repaid, Chance, and you know it. Friendships such as ours are never about who does what for whom, you know that as well. As far as the band goes, they're pretty mad and curious. On the other hand, the Gillette album is now #1 on BILLBOARD and I'd say there are no ways you'll be able to spend all of the money rushing in. The critics have been raving and calling it a classic already. The media is going nuts wondering about you. Now, what in Hell have you gotten into this time?" Luther said in his easy drawl.

Jessie stepped in and helped Chance to a lounge chair and then she addressed Luther.

"Have a seat where you can enjoy the view, Luther." She said. "It's just nine in the morning so I'm very hopeful that by the end of the day we'll all be much happier than we are right now."

"Ok, Chance, I repeat: What in the world have you done that could have destroyed you so completely?" Luther got right to the problem.

Their friend took a deep breath and began. "Well, before I go on with the latest mess I've created, I think you and I should let Jessie in on who we are and how come this friendship has lasted so long."

Luther nodded his assent.

"So here goes. Jess, I've told both of you my tale about being raised from the ages of 10 to 14 by the glorious Gertz couple. When I stopped the tales I told to you, I was 14 you may recall. It was good old Mother who entered that evening and made an astounding, and for me, very frightening announcement."

"She said: 'Paul, I've brought your supper as you see, and now I wish also to tell you that tonight will be your last in the terrible situation you have been kept. Father is away on business for a couple of days and you and I are going to change all.' She added gently. 'I have plans to remove you from this basement and out into the world again. There are some deadlines we have to meet so please eat you meal and then put your things in this back pack I have brought for you. Look around carefully and make sure you have anything you value as you will not be seeing us again forever I hope.'

"I know I saw tears in her eyes as she went on. She had planned the thing apparently for some time. I have never taken the time to investigate the hows and whys but I know that she came up with the dough and snuck me, the few clothes I had, my diary, my drawings, and my Gibson out of the dungeon. I learned later that old Andre was busy glad-handing whomever he could find to support his bid for election as Mayor of Branfield. The date would have been June 14, 1986 and I think we took off in her new Pontiac at 8PM. As she drove away she outlined the plan. I didn't even get a chance to look around the outside world there but I remember spending most of my time with the windows open and watching the cars go by, and taking in the houses and stores and screaming:

"Mother, what are we doing? Where are we going? Will you leave me somewhere? Where's Father? Does he know?"

She didn't pay any attention. All she said was, 'Paul, my son. This will be your only chance for a life. I will handle the consequences from here. Do not try to come back or contact anyone here. Please make the most of your life and be happy. I don't expect you to forgive Andre or me. I beg of you, make yourself forget us and this whole thing. You can't afford to let this horrible incident ruin your life.'

"Within an hour I would say, we arrived at what turned out to be a bus station. She ordered me out of the car, hugged me as if her own life were ending and then handed me a packet of instructions to help me navigate what she called my new life. I looked up and she was gone. I think I'd seen busses and cars when I was ten but still I was so afraid. Somehow I found a place to sit down and took out the information she had left me.

"Her note was not sentimental, just a straight list of things I should do right away. Gladys had seen to it that I was enrolled in a private high school for boys in Laramie, Wyoming. Her rules for my survival were intricate and meant to help a stranger in a strange place survive."

At this point, he handed out copies of the instructions.

1. Make sure you have your backpack and other belongings with you. Be sure to take good care of the guitar. It has always given you solace. You may need that in the next few years.

2. Take out the ticket you see in the red envelope and walk to the white booth about 15feet away. You'll notice it says: CHECK TICKETS HERE.

3. Listen well to the ticket taker for instructions. She or he will tell you which bus to get on. Make note of the number you are given. You are going to Laramie, Wyoming but your first bus will be going to DENVER COLORADO.

4. All busses will have a sign on their front to indicate their destination. Go directly to that bus as soon as you see it arrive.

5. The driver will take your ticket and punch a hole in it. Do not lose it as you will change busses in Denver, Colorado in about 7 hours and will go through this same routine in order to get to your final destination which will be LARAMIE, WYOMING.

6. The next bus will be marked Laramie, Wyoming.

7. Make sure you have your ticket and give it to the bus driver on that bus.

8. In about 5 more hours you will be told you are in Wyoming. You should get off in Laramie after making sure you have your backpack and guitar.

9. Look for a small bus labeled: HARLOW MILITARY PREP. Show the driver your enrollment identification which is in the blue envelope. You will soon arrive at the private secondary school that I have chosen. You will live there for the next four years.

10. I have already paid your tuition and sent clothes as well as two of the uniforms you will be wearing. I will be sending the school money for your needs as well as spending money as the months go on.

11. You will be welcomed at the school and assigned a roommate and room.

12. Please, Paul. Make the most of this opportunity. There are no apologies that would be enough to offer you for the treatment you have endured but I know you are strong, smart, and resilient.

13. DO NOT EVER TRY TO CONTACT ANYONE IN THIS AREA.

I will always love you, Gladys Gertz

"Somehow I managed to follow her directions and by noon the following day I was being shown my room and introduced to my roommate. I didn't know it but it was one of the luckiest things to ever happen to me. Luth, why don't you finish this part for me. I..." he hesitated and then turned away from his friends as the tears rolled again.

"OK. Chance, but I'll be brief. Yes, I was the roommate. I had been sent to HARLOW by my family in Los Angeles because they were so worried about the things I was getting involved in. You know: gangs, girls, drugs etc. I had thrown a fit about being sent away and at a cocky 15, in no mood to welcome some rube from New Hampshire which I called the sticks. What a pair we must have looked like! I was a runt compared to Chance, here. By the way, that was the name on his papers; birth certificate and school records: Morris George Chance. I don't know how she did it but in retrospect I suppose it wouldn't have hard for a long time town clerk. Anyway, I was maybe 5 feet and a half, decked out in gold chains and dreadlocks, and strutting around like a rooster while before me was this this blond-haired, skinny black kid who was obviously scared literally to death. I really do think I thought he was a 'dead kid walking'.

"I'm not going to go on and on about us. Let's just say the fact that we were both African-American actually played well for us. We liked each other immediately. I think he needed me to bolster his courage and I benefitted greatly from his wonder and quietness. It turned out that we both liked music. He was a wizard on the guitar. I swear he had taught it to be his friend and confidante. I now see that he

148

had not been allowed other outside interests. He was also widely educated and could recall more facts about history, science, and math than any teacher I had ever known. One thing I need to mention, he was a very talented artist. He could draw people and places as well as any sketch artist I've known. By the way, my friend, I never have seen the bunch you kept hidden under your mattress. Do you still have them?" When Chance didn't offer an answer, he continued.

"I noticed right away that he hated to be confined in any way. Our closet doors were always open. In the four years we were there he was never able to lock our room door. He let me do it if the powers that be ordered it but that's the only time. Now I know. My God, Chance, why didn't you say?" Luther said in anguish. Again there was no reaction.

"So we did OK at the school. We were the only black kids and became kind of courted, I guess. The teachers were impressed with Chance's knowledge and never questioned the papers Gladys had offered and because I came to admire his know-how so much I was spurred on to pay more attention as well. We also found that we both liked baseball so we played most of the years there. As he always did, even though he had never played the game he knew more about it in two days than Babe Ruth, I'd say. I never did grow a lot as you can see but he did. I was quick so the coach trained me to be the MUSTANGS short stop. As he rose to more than six feet he was some kind of good as a pitcher. We went on to the states in senior year but didn't make the nationals. Probably just as well because Chance was still pretty skittish about people he didn't know.

"In June 1990, instead of going to graduation ceremonies the two of us visited the school's dean and managed to get copies of our grades and a real diploma to send to my folks. We then packed everything we had and put it into a rental in Laramie and headed for the nearest ARMY Recruiting Center. Before we could blink, I think, we were in the United States Army and were trained as JASCO, a joint assault signal company. It was a joint service unit that provided ship to

149

shore, air to ground communications to coordinate and control Naval Gunfire and Close Air Support to the troops. Bingo! The next thing we knew we were standing in sand in the DESERT STORM thing. We did OK. There was an explosion that happened from which I would never have survived without Chance."

"Let's not go there." injected Chance.

Luther continued, "Neither of us had anyone else who cared much so in 1994 with a medal or two we decided to opt out and with our papers in hand headed off to be regular citizens." He paused, lost in thought.

"Wow. Some life, huh? OK, Chance it's your turn. Give us a couple of sentences about who we are now." He said as he patted his friends arm, then poured another cup of coffee and took a seat.

All three of them sat in silence, two of them wondering what to expect, one wondering if he could go on.

"I should have known you'd give me the good part." Chance began. "So Jessie, I imagine you haven't guessed who we are as yet? Probably been too busy making your own life to notice musicians, and I'd say you've done one heck of a job. As for us, once out of the service we both settled down in a rental in the Los Angeles area."

"As we have mentioned we soon found that we both loved music. I loved playing the guitar and Luther here couldn't have been a better audience. He knew some people here and there and it didn't take long for him to con me into thinking we could form a band. In fact, along the way he introduced me to a friend of his who was struggling to make a living as a drummer in the California area. From the late 1990's until this past June we've been trying to be successful in the music business and have done pretty damn well. First of all Luth found me a job playing in a pub five nights a week. People seemed to enjoy what I did and I must admit I almost believed I had some worth. Then he heard a little band in another part of town and invited them to meet me and maybe see if there was something we could do together. It turned out that Dave Gregg was a wondrous drummer and the guy who played keys, Peter Smith, couldn't be matched. The three of us jammed it out for nearly a week always after our own jobs were finished. I don't know if I have ever been so tired or enthused about anything before or since. Luther was totally committed and immediately asked them if they'd be interested in forming a new group. He said he knew some people who might be interested and if not he'd find us gigs. We believed him because we were so glad to have someone to handle any business that might come our way. Imagine! After one week at our new place some guy named Chuck Harden came up and announced that he was a bass guitarist and would like to join us. A few days later he ambled in to rehearsal followed by another bearded wonder holding an alto sax. The sax player shook hands and said his name was Randall Masters but he liked to be called Rand. Two months later after much haggling over a name CHANCE AND THE STRAGGLERS was off on their first outing and Luther was our manager. That was it. We have never looked back."

Jessie jumped from her seat. "That's it! I knew I'd seen you somewhere. I think it was in Long Island or maybe New Jersey. I...You guys are the most popular band practically in the world! Wow! What do I do now? How am I to react?" She said like a kid. "Can I have your autograph? Should I be throwing my underwear at you?"

The sadness disappeared. The three of them began laughing and hugging. For a millisecond, all was right with the world.

"You know what? We've wiled away the whole morning. Let's take a breather. Morris, why don't you go out on the deck and enjoy some of this wonderful air? Luther and I will amble around the estate and then we'll have some lunch and if you're ready we'll attack whatever it is that needs attacking. OK? Just give me a minute to arrange my life with Gene down stairs." Jessie returned within minutes, announcing that she had taken the next 6 days off.

Morris started to object and argue but was far too tired. He was asleep in the sun within minutes. Luther and Jessie headed out to look her estate over and then planned to prepare something to eat for later.

BEVERLY A. MASSEY

CHAPTER XIV
A WAY OUT

By 5 o-clock in the afternoon Luther and Jessie could be found in the kitchen bustling around making hors d'oeuvres hoping to help Chance settle down and realize that he needed to waken and face his music. They had had a fine afternoon learning about each other and both adding more facts to their friend's horrendous tale of his youth. Neither could really believe that such a thing might happen but there had been others recently that were nearly as bad. They marveled at the story of a Jaycee Dugard who was kept in a man's back yard for nearly 20 years and revisited the Elizabeth Smart saga as well. There were many others, predominantly young women, but they were sure many young boys had been similarly treated. The underlying reason for most of the kidnappings was sexual. But this one was something they could not imagine. This one seemed to be for selfish political reasons, coupled with undying love. Why in the world would a successful businessman and well known entrepreneur like Andre Jan Gertz do such a thing? Was he really as much of a narcissist as it would appear? And, why in the world would a wife cooperate?

"You don't have to live in a big city to see nut-cakes, you know." Luther began "I know we hear of shocking city crime each day but here we are; in New Hampshire...in a small city and our friend...Oh, Hi Chance. I didn't see you come back into the house. How are you feeling? Better? We've had a fine time touching bases and if we are able to fix this mess, Alice and I will be able to have you two over for dinner. You know since we've split the band up and the kids are in college in Boston, she and I have taken a condo on the coast down in Provincetown."

"Sounds good to me." interrupted Jessie. "But first, what can I get you? Would you like a drink or maybe a burger? It will only take a minute. We've whipped up a few munchies here but you might want something more substantial. God! Morris. I'm babbling, here. Sit down. What do you want or wish for?"

"How about I just shoot myself?" Morris said quietly, and then looked straight into their eyes. "OK, you two. I don't have any right to involve either of you in my catastrophe and it ends here. I will be off in a minute and beg you both to move on. Pretend you have never heard my story and let me try to disappear. Thanks for the shelter and the support.

"Once in my younger days I remember being blown away by the sound of Mother saying that I should be patient and she would fix it. I recall I had read some book about joy and how happy the feeling of it could warm one's heart. I thought that if she did what she said she could do, I would feel it-the joy of freedom. She pulled it off too late. The feeling didn't come. Now, here you guys are. You have given me a lease on life. I now know what joy is. Give me a hug, I'm off and running." With that he picked up his guitar and small back-pack and started for the door.

"SIT DOWN IN THAT GOD DAMNED CHAIR." Luther spoke louder than he ever had then faced off not two feet away from his friend. "If you think we are going to let you go you're crazier than you appear. SIT, CHANCE. I know you're bigger than me but you'll feel my fist any minute."

"Stop it, you two." Jessie's voice broke as she spoke. "Both of you sit down. Let's get to the meat of this thing. Morris, I guess I'll start to call you Chance from now on so...Here you two. I've made a fancy cocktail and we're going to hash this out and we're going to eat the food and we're..."she began to sob. Both men sat as ordered. Minutes passed and then Chance began:

"As you both know, I have been hugely successful in most things I have done. Luther kept me sane in good old HARLOW MILITARY PREP, and the two of us propped each other up in the U.S. Army. On top of that we're both members of one of the most famous rock bands in the world. Jessie you've had to claw your way up after giving up your mother's lawyer wish for you and you've done a fine job, too. I'm sure if I investigated a bit I would find some rough times in your lives. It happens to us all. You two are doing just fine.

"But me? I have not handled my years in the cage very well. I have allowed a crazy couple of people in my past to wreck every step I've made up the ladder of happiness. I haven't been able to forget, to forgive, or to stop the nightmares that have plagued me. I hesitate to tell you this but, over the past weeks I have gone ahead and taken steps to remedy the situation.

"Now, before I tell my story I say once again. I have money. I can disappear into some foreign country or somewhere and you'll never need to know. I will not blame either of you if you pack up and go right now. What I have done is probably a felony." At this Jessie gasped and started to leave the room.

"Aw, shit, Chance. Couldn't you have found some other way than..." as he spoke, Luther turned his head in order to avoid having his best friend see his anguish. Then both he and Jessie sat back down.

155

"No. No. Don't sit, turn away. This is really serious. Most people would and should leave and let me finish it." Chance sat down and took a large swallow of the drink Jessie had offered then waited. Luther would say later that he was sure he heard the electric clock on the wall tick.

"I have never in my life had to make such a decision." Luther said. "I'm thinking about Alice and the kids. They're 18 and 19 now, you know. I...I tell you what. Before you begin I'm going to call Alice and meander around the river out there. When I get back you'll have my answer." He was gone before either of the others made a move.

"OK, here's what I think." Jessie pronounced as she brought him a plate. "I've never been as happy as I have been in the last few days. Though I would have scoffed at such a notion just a day or so ago, I feel that I've met someone I could spend my life with. So, I guess that means that I need to stick with this devil through thick and thin. I'm not leaving. I will stand by you no matter what. I still have some legal experts in my past. If needed, I could call for advice. Look. You must eat something. Grab one of these crab cakes Luther made and I'll get you another drink." Within an hour Luther was back.

"That looks great, Jessie. How about a dish for me? And then I have something to say."

Once they were settled, he began. "Chance it doesn't matter what you have done. I would not desert you if you killed one or both of your wondrous parents. I hope that's not true but whatever it is both Alice and I are prepared to back you up. We might not be able to forgive you but we will never desert you. All for one etc. etc. so let's hear it and don't spare the details."

Chance cleared his throat and allowed his words to begin. "Before we wound up the Gillette thing I had hired a detective to check on things in Branfield. You know, where Gladys and Andre were living, what they were up to, and how did the town see them. It didn't take long as they are both public figures in the little berg.

"As far as the town went, Andre was just what the movers and shakers wanted him to be. He had managed to get more and more legislation passed which prohibited any undesirables (meaning poor, black, or probably Democrats), much chance at living in their paradise. Many were suspicious of how this was done but hadn't raised questions for fear of retribution. Gladys had just retired at the age of 77. Andre was now 78 and thinking of running for the state Senate. There was some question in the electorate as to whether or not he was too old but none that I heard objected to Gladys as mayor. I was quite amazed at the trust they put in her but I guess they would have had no way of knowing... I'm sorry, guys give me a minute." With that he stepped out onto the terrace again and wrestled with his thoughts.

"OK. Here goes. In the past weeks I have disguised myself and taken time to learn a lot about Branfield. I quickly discovered that it was still a small town at heart. Small towns love to gossip I guess, because it didn't take but a day or two to see that Andre and Gladys were their prized citizens. It appears that Andre was to be feared but Gladys was pitied and trusted. From what I can remember, I would have assumed this to be the case.

"My disguise was probably unnecessary as I had been kept completely under wraps so to speak when I lived there. No one seemed to be interested in me so I took more time to find the house of horrors and guess what? There it was just where Google had said. And, just up the street about a half mile or so there was GERTZ MANOR. I put my plans in motion about 3 weeks ago, just before disbanding THE SCRAGGLERS.

"I knocked at the door of my home/cage one day and found a pretty single mother of two kids anxious to sell and start a new life way away from the old town. It was easy to handle. I hired a good real-estate firm in Rhode Island to negotiate terms and within a week the place belonged to Morris George Chance. I took over the house and immediately found the secret to opening my home away from home of many years ago. God!

157

"I kept to myself, arriving only for weekends and even then kept blinds drawn and made no attempt to go into town. Once I had my ducks 'rowed' as they might say, I was ready. I had found time to dismantle all of the security sensors old Andre had had installed on his estate and one night around 10pm, I believe it was two days after I talked to the boys in the band I arrived at the MANOR, rang the bell and there stood MOTHER."

At this point Chance described in detail where he stood. He had his captors caged and/or broken. He had the town believing the pair was on hiatus in order to decide what to do with the rest of their lives. He assumed that at this moment Andre had an essay ready for his perusal and hoped that he had already gagged at the sight of oatmeal and peanut butter sandwiches. His final description of the choices he had given Gladys made both Jessie and Luther throw their hands in horror.

"You did what?" whispered Luther in disbelief. "You can't be serious."

"My God, Chance. Why? Why such a dangerous game? Has your life been so meaningless that you can't picture it being happy? I'm blown away." Jessie cried through clenched teeth.

"A gun? With a bullet? To a couple of maniacs? What the hell, Chance. It would be hard for me right now to tell which of the three of you is the most unhinged." Luther stated. "Shit, Chance." With that he opened the sliders and took a patio seat, his head in his hands.

Dead silence filled the whole house. Chance seemed to be in some other world while Jessie had begun constantly shaking her head. After an hour or so, sick of the time ticking away, Jessie rose and rallied the two men.

"OK. Listen up. I want each to think honestly as we discuss this thing. And there's to be no holding back because we like each other, or because we feel bad about the situation, or...whatever.

"Chance, you put this thing in motion so it's time for you to act like it. Make notes if you wish but I have a few questions I believe we must consider here." Jessie said in her best legal voice.

"Number 1, When are you due back at the old homestead?

Number 2: What do you expect to find when you get there?

Number 3: What payoff would make you feel better?

Number 4: Luth, do you still want to help here? If so, who do you know who can help? Any really good psychiatrists?

Number 5: Chance, where are those original drawings you made so many years ago?

Finally, Number 6: Did you by any chance keep the original instructions Gladys gave you when you left Branfield on that bus or the stuff from the army?

"Luther, once we've answered these questions, we need to get on with it and offer up whatever we can think of that might help Jack the Ripper here, to get out of this mess. All of us need to take some time to think about what to do. Lath you take the terrace, Chance head for the bedroom and I'll stay right here. Now, Go! We'll talk in one hour."

In exactly one hour Jessie blew a whistle and ordered the men in to discuss their thoughts.

"First I think we all can agree that this is a dangerous mess. My understanding is that you are due back at 6am tomorrow morning. It is now 4pm. If we add in an hour's travel, we now have 13 hours to consolidate a plan. Right?" Both men nodded and Jess went on... "So, let's do the easy thing first. Chance, where are those drawings you made right now?"

"Ah, I've got a safe deposit box in the Providence Bank Of America. The original of those, the school stuff, and the bus trip are

159

there." I have given folders with copies to each of my captives." Chance answered.

"Fine, that will do. Have you got any more of the copies with you?" Chance nodded.

"OK. That's one down, now, to the more disastrous aspects of your life. What do you expect to see when you arrive tomorrow?"

"I think I'll find them sitting in their respective places, wondering what to do." Chance said quietly.

"And, what would you like to find when you arrive? Andre, with pages of essays and two books read? Gladys happily cooking apple pie for all? What, Chance?" Jessie said angrily.

"I don't know anymore." mumbled Chance. "I was just so angry. I guess I wasn't thinking of a future."

Luther could not tolerate the tension between his two best friends.

He stood and said. "Look you two. Calm down. I haven't come up with one good thought. We already know what's important here. I'd say its Chance's mental stability and the opportunity for both of you to live a long happy life; none of which will happen if the gun is out of the cage. Therefore I suggest that we all go to Branfield right now and somehow fix this."

"No way. That would probably be suicide if I've read Andre correctly. The more I think about it the more sure I am that Gladys will take number 3. So, that means I need to be the only one in danger. I'll leave now." Chance said as he stood.

Luther said quietly. "Somehow, Chance, you seem to have forgotten what it means to be a real friend or parent. Either means that you are not alone. Why in the world do you not understand that you have a person or persons who will carry you when you can no longer carry yourself? Have we not made any dent in that armor of yours? I think maybe it's time for you to trust again. If we try I think the three of us can try to make this all go away."

"You're right, Luther." Jess agreed. "Let's think a bit longer. Is there any sense to our calling the local police or a lawyer? Remember, we have the drawings and the other papers. Maybe a jury would forgive you for this mess you've made Chance."

"Oh, I don't think so. One whiff of this scandal and the paparazzi would be all over us." Luther said. "You may not realize what a big deal this would be. Imagine. THE MOST LOVED AND SUCCESSFUL BAND LEADER IN THE WORLD IMPRISONS THE MAYOR OF BRANFIELD, NH. It would be disastrous."

"OK, then. What do you think is best, Luther?" Jessie said.

"I say again. Let's get going. If Chance is correct, nothing will have happened. If Gladys has had her way then they're gone and good riddance. If they are both there and undecided what to do maybe we can make some kind of a deal to just stop this whole thing. What we need to do is figure out a way for the three of us to get into the house without the whole town knowing it."

"That's not a real problem." Chance offered. "I've let it be known that I've bought the property for a friend and that I'm fixing it up. They've seen me coming and going in my trusty Toyota for a few weeks and I'm sure the town wags have spread the news. I don't think there will be an eye blink if I arrive today. You understand they don't know who I am so I will have to get into my disguise. If we do this you'd want to look like a workman, Luth, and Jess, maybe a bit less beautiful. It could be dangerous you know. There is a loaded gun in that cage and she might have figured a way to get at it. By the way, remember the gun only has one bullet."

"We're all in. Let's get going." came from Chance's two friends.

"I'm off for a few to get a carpenters stuff." Luther offered. "Be back in 15."

"I'll just go get my working jeans, a couple of half full cans of paint and a sweatshirt. That should let me pass as helper number two." Jess added, and they were gone.

BEVERLY A. MASSEY

CHAPTER XV

THE POT IS ABOIL

Chief Rollins arose at 5am on Tuesday June 21. He managed a few push-ups and a couple of cups of coffee and then hauled out his tablet to check his phone and his day. There had not been any problems in Branfield during the night apparently and his second in command had sent a text message that all was quiet and controlled. The thought crossed his mind to call in sick and then contact Octavia. They could have a fine trip up the coast and stop at that restaurant in Wiscasset, Maine. The dream expanded as he took his shower and heard the weather report on WBZ. Fair, 89', no rain.

"Watch it old man." He said aloud. "You sound like you'd like this to go much further." He had to admit that seemed like a great choice; maybe he'd approach her tonight.

By 6am, the three conspirators arrived in Branfield and headed for 565 Pine St. As expected, there were very few cars about. Most seemed to be everyday commuters headed for work and not paying a great deal of attention. Chance cruised down Pine St., past the great gated manor and then pulled up at their destination.

"This is not a bad little house." Luther spoke first.

"Yeah, it's too bad I never saw it until the last few weeks." Chance answered.

"Look, Chance. This could be ended right here. Are you sure you want to go in there? Luther and I could go and set them free, you know. Then we could all high tail it and just forget the whole thing happened. Face it. They know you have the drawings to ruin them. I think they'd be glad to make some kind of a deal. I feel so strongly that there could be real trouble right here if you go in." Jess said gently but urgently.

"Moot suggestion, Jess. Look over across the street; right there under that big oak. I'd say the jig is already up. Here we go, Chance. Hands in the air." Luther spoke quietly but firmly as they saw Branfield's Police Chief alight from his car door.

"My God! Take a look down the street by the manor. Here comes another car. An SUV full of women. At this ungodly hour? What in the world? Are we bugged or something?" Jess added ominously.

"I don't know and I don't really care." Chance said. "I came here to end this thing and that's just what I'm going to do." With that, he leapt from the car, ran to the front door, and entered the house.

The SUV drew slowly up to Jim Rollins as he started to cross the street.

"Octavia! What the devil are you three doing out at this hour? And, why here? It looks like Route 95 to me." Jimmy said as he opened the car's door. "Are there any more people you plan on meeting here?"

"It's a long story Jimmy." Octavia began. "I told l you we've been trying to get an appointment to speak to Andre for quite a while and couldn't get a meeting set up so we decided to try to catch him early and maybe get an interview. This was the day. We drove by and rang the bell but no one seems home..."

"Interview? The whole town has seen his notice; the one that said he and Gladys had some stuff to settle or whatever. What makes you think he'll see you three? Why do you want to speak to him anyway? Are you into politics now? Have you and your old pals nothing better to do?"

"Well, we are interested in the rumor that he intends to run for state senate and that probably Gladys will run for mayor. We've been studying the politics of the town and we're not at all satisfied with the way things have gone. Have you thought about the fact that only the rich and white are living here now? Why is that? Is somebody's pocket getting fuller?" said Marion.

"Should we entrust any more of our children's and grandchildren's future to people like Andre Jan and Gladys Gertz?" Martha added. "What about your family? I know they have always felt they needed to provide affordable housing around here. They've been tied up every time they suggest building less expensive housing or a few apartments in town. Have they given that up? Is that the way we want to go?"

"By the way James," Marion slipped in. "What are you doing hiding over there under the trees at such an hour?"

"I'll be dammed. Who would have thought that at 6am on a Monday morning, I'd be asked to give an opinion on such goings on? You know, Olivia, that Adam upped and left town a couple of weeks ago. I was concerned. I got a text from him last night. He just wanted me to know that he'd decided to go into the Army and had been assigned to a base in Texas. They're really anxious to have more troops who have his expertise given the Ukraine thing. I have to say I thought it was a good idea. He could use some more discipline. Maybe you three could use some too. Would you like the Navy better? Maybe the Marines?" he said harshly and then went on.

"Adam also suggested that I might want to meet the new owner of Andre's old homestead. He sounded kind of mysterious but not urgent and it was quiet down at the station so I came along over to say

165

hello. Now I've found a bunch of ladies hankering for an audience with the mayor. Marion, does Hal know what you're up to? I think we should call a family meeting and talk about this before you get more involved. By the way I just saw the guy who bought this place heading in. He had a woman and a man who looked like contractors with him. The woman looked just like that woman who owns JESSIE'S. I guess I'll go along and you probably should too."

As he spoke, a loud bang from the inside of the house splintered the air.

"Get into your car and move. Now!" Jim shouted as he drew his gun. "Call the station and tell them to send Carl immediately."

"OK" Octavia said to her companions. "Hang on we're out of here."

Martha grabbed her seat belt and told Marion to call the station. The KIA left a dust path down the street then they parked near the manor. Within ten minutes, Branfield's Deputy Chief, raced past them. They sat in their catbird seat waiting for the next event.

The police chief rang the bell and pounded on the door to no avail. Just as he and Carl were ready to break in, the door swung open and there stood the young woman they had seen with the paint cans.

"Can I help you, officer?" Jessica asked.

"Help us? What are you talking about, Ma'am.'' Jim spoke. "I'm sure I heard a gunshot a minute ago and...'

"My God!" Jessie screamed. "I was vacuuming and didn't hear a thing. Should I be running or hiding or...what is going on here?"

"Good morning chief. Yes, I heard the shot as well. I think it came from the wine cellar down below." Luther said calmly as he appeared from a back room. "Let's go see what is going on."

Suddenly, Chance appeared from the cellar door. "No. That's not how this is going." He said. "I guess the best thing would be for you to follow me and bring your recorder. This will take a while and I feel it's got to end today. I..." His voice wavered and the chief caught him just as he began to tumble backwards.

166

"Chance! Oh no. Chance!" shouted Jessie. "Luther do something. He's bleeding a lot. Do something one of you."

"Wait a minute; I'll give the orders here. You, get on the damn phone and order an ambulance." Jim Rollins ordered Carl, and then handed Chance over to Luther. Luth grabbed Chance and placed him on the near floor.

"And you, stop your hysterics and give me a clue" he said to Jessie. "Why are you all here?? And, who the devil are you? For some reason, I think you're the woman who owns JESSIE'S. I think I've seen this guy before." as he looked the wounded man over. "Who is he?"

"This is going to take a while, Chief." Luther offered. "I think you need to leave Jessie here to deal with the EMT crew and come with me to the wine cellar. I have no idea what you'll see but I guess I'd order another cop from your roster if I was you. I don't believe there's any more ammo down there but you never know."

As the EMT's arrived, Jessie took over with Chance and Luther started for the cellar stairs.

"What do you mean? Is there some reason there is someone else in this house that might have a gun? What the hell is going on? What's your name?"

"My name is Luther Banks. The guy who has been injured is Morris George Chance. He's the leader of the band, CHANCE AND THE STRAGGLERS. I'm their manager. You may have heard of them- they have been very successful worldwide. The rest of the story will develop as we get through this terrible day. Let's start by taking a look downstairs. I'd recommend you have your pistol at the ready and your curiosity really sharp."

At this point Chance was being treated by the emergency crew loudly announcing that he would not go to any hospital. Chief Rollin's next in command, Lt. Davis, entered and went directly to his commander.

"What's up, chief? Is this a neighborhood spat or should I call more of the squad in?"

"I really have no idea, Carl. But the more I do learn the more bizarre it seems. This is Luther Banks here. He's going to try to clear this thing up. I do know that the guy who was just hauled outside is a world famous guitar player if that means anything. Apparently, he's the guy we've been seeing off and on around town. Hal's wife Marion as well as Dr. Dennis' wife and Octavia have all been trying to find out who he is for the past few weeks. They've been pestering me but I have no idea." With that he turned to Luther.

"OK, then, Luther Banks, let's hit the cellar stairs. We already have one person shot at, so Carl, have your gun ready. I'm told we may need to use them." Jim Rollins spoke as he drew his own.

The wine cellar was quiet and musty-cool. Its shelves were dusty and held only a few bottles. As the chief surveyed the place it appeared to have been deserted long ago. That is with the exception of the furthest edge of the bottom shelf. There was no dust on the last two feet or so and he watched carefully as Luther reached beneath the board and pressed some kind of button. The shelves began to rotate, stopping at a 90' angle. The three men were stunned at what they saw before them. There in a small room sat Gladys Gertz. The town clerk held a Colt 45 in her lap, while before her locked in a cage of steel, sat Mayor Andre Jan Gertz. No one spoke. No one moved. The silence in the room was unbelievable. Lieutenant Davis was the first to get his bearings.

"Uh, Mrs. Gertz, Are there any bullets left in the gun you have on your lap?" Lt. Davis said carefully. Gladys shook her head back and forth but didn't speak. "Alright then, would you please hand me that gun you have?" Gladys did so and then he went on. "Do you know if there are other weapons in this house?"

"I doubt it sir. This was just part of my son's plans I guess. I have made a terrible mistake and I expect to pay for it. Just put the cuffs on, I have no intent to resist." At this she held out her wrists as if she had done so before.

Jim and Carl were speechless. Finally they began to look the room over and tried to make sense of what they could see. There was a room-sized steel-barred cage before their eyes and within that sat an apoplectic man-Branfield's mayor!

"Carl, do you have a recorder in your car? Or maybe a camera? If so, go get them. If not, call Dick from the switchboard and tell him to bring you one. And, I want this whole situation kept under wraps. Do not speak one word about this place until we know more. Do not use sirens. From now on don't touch anything in this room or the stairway. I'd say this is a crime scene and we need to be careful." The chief commanded

Lt. Davis left immediately and Chief Rollins continued:

"Mayor Gertz. What is going on here? Who shot Morris Chance? Why? Where do you fit in and, why here? What is this little cage doing over here and what do those two keys fit?"

"I have nothing to say except, get me out of here, Chief, and you can consider that an order." Andre spoke with authority. "And if you insist on continuing to ask questions, I want my lawyer, now." With that, he moved from his bed to his desk and sat regally in the small chair.

"Are you not interested in your own wife's safety? Ms. Gertz, can you give us any information? At least tell us if there are any more dangerous people in the house?"

Gladys shook her head. The police chief wondered if she'd ever speak again. Suddenly, Chance and Jessie came into the room accompanied by Lt. Paul, his camera, and a small tape recorder.

"Luth, Chance was lucky." Jessie announced. "He was grazed just to the right of his heart and the Emergency crew has patched him up. They felt that he should be admitted but he has refused, and..."

Luther interrupted with, "Thank God, Chance. Now these good people are going to need a lot of explaining and I would advise that you call our lawyers before you make any statements."

"Not necessary, Chief. I can tell you all you need to know. This ruffian you see before you broke into my new home a couple of lifetimes ago and has brought my poor wife and I here to torture us. He

169

has been ordering and threatening Gladys for days and when push came to shove she grabbed the gun from that cage and tried to kill him. Too bad she didn't, I say. I want him arrested right this minute and then let's get those keys over there in the cage and get me out of this dungeon." Andre Jan said taking charge.

"Do you agree with your husband, Ms. Gertz?" Carl stepped in. "And how about you, Mr. Chance?"

Silence fell over the room. No one seemed to be able to offer any explanation.

"Alright, then. Carl, we'll need five pair of handcuffs and I'd say one more vehicle. I'm taking the whole crew here down to headquarters for questioning and we'll go from there. I'll also want this place and the Manor put under lock and key and guarded until further notice. Be specific: NO ONE is to enter either house unless they have permission from me. Let's get Herm and Donny back in right now. They will be responsible for keeping my orders followed. And as for you, keep your information to yourself. This will be a field day for the press. Stress this to all members of the police force: Anyone other than me anyone who speaks to the press will be fired."

"Understood, Chief." Lt. Davis saluted and was gone. Chief Rollins made one more phone call and then proceeded to cuff all of the participants.

"You've got to be kidding. You're going to arrest me, the victim here, and trot us down through town??? Not in my lifetime. You have my statement and that should be enough. Open this damn cage NOW." Andre shouted.

A small voice entered the silent room.

"I have something to say and I don't need a lawyer." Gladys spoke. "This is really all my fault. I have allowed it to go on way too long." Then she sat down and commenced. "The story began many years ago when I first met Andre. It is long and complicated but bottom line, I instigated the near destruction of a boy and now he has tried to save me. Is there some place where we could discuss this?" Gladys said in her raspy quiet voice, and then turned to Chance.

"Paul Richard Medford or Morris George Chance, or Paul Gertz, whatever you choose to call yourself now, you have exceeded all of my hopes and dreams for you. I'm so glad to see that you are alright. I will fix it now without even wanting or expecting your forgiveness. I will not even consider asking God to help me. Now, chief, could I please begin?"

"Chief Rollins, I guess it is time for all of us to settle this. I think you need to make a decision as to how to deal with this mess." Chances stepped in. "I would suggest that you leave your mayor under guard and locked up just where he is."

"Well, maybe. I do know this, there's been some kind of bizarre crime here and I need to get my detectives in here so please, nobody touch anything. Carl, I called the state bureau when I first got here. They are sending help. I will leave you in charge of the state crime scene investigators when they get here. In the meantime, I'm going to take this motley bunch upstairs and see what we have. Remember whatever the Mayor tries to get you to do you need to clear with me. Yes? Oh, and give me the recorder. I have a feeling this is going to be a doozie."

"Yes sir." Carl said with a salute.

Chief Jim rounded Gladys, Luther, Jessie, and Chance up and headed for the stairs.

"You'll regret this Jimmy." howled Andre. "I'll have your badge in a heartbeat."

CHAPTER XVI

FILLING IN THE BLANKS

The silver KIA had drawn up just past GERTZ MANOR. "Octave, I thought I heard Jimmy say we should get far away." Martha exclaimed. "Didn't he say there had been gun shots or at least one gun shot?"

"I darn well heard it that way." Marion chimed in. "What are you up to?"

"Well. He doesn't know it but I had a police scanner installed in the car when we got back together. It gives me a chance to know what's going on and I feel better knowing he's safe. Yes, I did hear what sounded like a gunshot and here's the best way for us to catch up on what's happening. I'll turn it on and Jimmy will never know."

The radio kicked in immediately. It appeared that the chief was giving orders to his Lieutenant. He gave very few details but announced that he was on his way and would expect Carl Davis to hold the fort at the mystery man's home.

"Look down there!" Marion spoke up. "I see the EMT truck and also a black sedan. Looks like an unmarked detective to me. You know, that's what all of the shows on TV use."

"You think so? Well, there goes the emergency vehicle; no flashing lights or sirens, so I guess all is OK. Do you think we should go and introduce ourselves?"

"No. No. No. Octavia. This seems a big deal to me. Let's just try the manor door again and maybe Andre the great will fill us in." Martha said.

"Oh, I don't know. I think I've lost my interest in our Mayor and his wife. This getting up so early is not for me. Let's head for my house and I'll make some breakfast and just let this play out. We know Andre and Gladys have only a couple more weeks of energizing themselves so we'll attack the politics then." Marion offered.

"Great idea Mae, I'm not into this either. We probably have better fish to fry. I'm supposed to babysit this afternoon and I can't wait." Martha agreed. "Start this thing up and let's leave it to Jimmy; whatever it is."

"Some detectives you two are." Octavia said. "But I guess you're right. Leaving good enough alone as my mother always said no doubt is the better way. I want to tell you though, that painter we saw entering the house looked exactly like Jessie Gilmore the woman who owns the little bar and grill Jimmy and I have adopted."

With that they three sleuths left for to go back to their everyday lives.

It was not the same for the 'criminals' who faced Chief Rollins and the State investigators. The chief had settled them down in the small living room, still handcuffed, He apologized but said there were many things to clear up before anyone would be charged or freed.

"Let's begin, people. This man is a detective from the State Attorney's Office in Concord. I will ask you each in turn to state your name and current address, phone number, and employment. Then Det. Cahill will begin his questions. I want you to realize that everything any of you or anyone else in this room have to say at least until we dismiss or charge you, is being recorded. Is that understood?" All nodded. "You need to say your answer vocally." He added.

"Let it be known that all four suspects in the room spoke a resounding 'YES'. We'll start with you, Luther. Then Chance, Jessie, and Gladys."

"My name is Luther Banks." Luth began. "My address is 2367 Alamo Dr., San Diego, California. My phone number is: 333-455-9123. I am the manager of the band, CHANCE AND THE STRAGGLERS."

"My name is Morris George Chance." Chance stated. "I am currently living at: 595 Pine St., Branfield, NH. My phone number is: 858-975-0034. I am the founder and lead guitarist of the band, CHANCE AND THE STRAGGLERS."

"My name is Jessica Ann Gilmore. I am the owner of JESSIE'S BAR AND GRILL, located at 277 Apple Way, Greenview, NH. This is also my residence address. My phone number is: 612-342-0665."

"My name is Gladys Morgan Medford Gertz. My address is 600 Pine St., Branfield, NH. My phone number is 761-237-9002. I am currently employed by the city of Branfield, NH as their Town Clerk and Office Manager.

With no pause for a breath, Gladys continued. "If I may gentlemen, I know I can spare everyone a lot of anguish and time. I assure you this is my fault. Whatever Andre has done I have been a party to, and it has been grievous. We are both guilty. At this time I would like to tell the whole story and let the chips fall where they may."

"Would there be any objection to this?" Detective Charles Cahill asked? Do you want a lawyer, Mrs. Gertz? Do any of the rest of you want to call one?" Let it be known each of the people in the room said: 'Not at this time.'"

"No? At this time, June 27, 2022, I, Detective Charles Cahill, of the New Hampshire State Police, declare that the following is Gladys

Morgan Medford Gertz of Bradfield, NH, recounting events from the last 42 years."

"Now then let's hear what you have to say Mrs. Gertz." He added as he handed her the mike.

"I was born and raised in Branfield, NH. My parents were older when I came into the world. They were very unsure of how to raise a child and so were overprotective. I was very shy all through school. I was often needed at home to help my elderly parents and so didn't really make many friends in high school. As a result, I was unhappy with my life and always planned one day to leave our small town and maybe even travel the world.

"After I graduated from BHS I went down state to further my education. My plan then was to find employment in New York City and travel a bit. Once again, it was not to be. My dad died of a sudden heart attack on the day I graduated and I was needed at home.

"I was upset but stayed home and eventually landed a job as a clerk at our town offices. I cared for my mother for years and also was successful at my job and within the last 30 years have been promoted to the position of Office Manager as well as the Town Clerk.

"In 1980, I met and began to date Andre Jan Gertz. Most of you would know of his successes, I'm sure. I freely admit I fell completely in love and within a year we were making wedding plans. Once again a problem came up just after we made our announcement.

"The next day my mother passed away. In addition, within a week, her sister called from Hartford, Connecticut and asked if I could help her. I know her story has been heard many times before. Her wayward daughter had fallen in with a bad crowd and had become a drug addict. In addition, she had a 4 year old child and could not care for him. Aunt Helen took him in, giving him a safe home for six years. Now, my aunt was aging and needed to move to a rest home. She could not care for what was then a 12 year old and asked me to take him in. What could I say? I said of course. Andre said no way unless I would be willing to allow him to educate the boy without interference.

176

"I could not imagine life without Andre any more than I could imagine not having a son to care for, so I agreed. We married and then brought Paul Richard Medford into this home on Pine St. while our new home was being built. I was so happy to have a son I cannot tell you.

"That is, until the first day he arrived and Andre shocked me beyond words. He announced that Paul would be kept in a locked room for at least 2 years, maybe more, depending on how he behaved and learned to follow rules. Next he took us both to the wine cellar and on through behind it where you have all been. Andre had seen to it that the cage you have seen behind the wine cellar was built and stocked. I have no idea why I acquiesced. Exhaustion? Love-blind? If I look at myself today, I still cannot believe the choice I made.

"Once Paul was locked inside Andre handed us both a folder containing our responsibilities for the foreseeable future. Essentially, Paul was to read, learn advanced math, geography, and whatever else Andre suppled. After which he was to write a report and submit it to Andre by the following morning. I was assigned to be my son's keeper. I was shocked but still thought that I could fix it somehow. I was sure my love for him would be strong enough to stop the madness. I was wrong.

"As you know, I have hung on to this marriage for many years. Andre and I have been very successful business-wise but I fear we failed miserably at what really matters. Finally, through deception, I did see to it that when Paul reached the age of 14, in June 1986, I was able to remove him from the cage and send him away where he would be safe. You will have to ask Paul how much of his past years he wishes to divulge. Andre was furious but realized that he needed my influence to accomplish his political goals. We have lived in separate camps for years.

"I had not seen nor heard from Paul in all of this time until last week when he arrived at the manor and started his revenge. Actually, I think his plan was just what we deserved. As you can see, Andre was caged and I was to be his jailer. I have copies of his to do list which I can supply you. It is really only a copy of the one my husband insisted on when Paul joined us.

"Now, in 2022, Paul, now known as Chance, has insisted that the only way out of the cage he put us in was for Andre to read a few books on self-improvement, child rearing, and good human behavior. He decided that forcing his vicious step father to do this would chase away the nightmares he has apparently always had. Andre refused to cooperate in any way and even thought he could break Chance just by being obstinate.

"After two days of Andre's failure to follow rules, Paul then brought in the little cage with the gun and keys inside. When he left a few days ago, he gave me the code to open it leaving it to me to decide what should happen next. I could free Andre and go to the police. I could get the gun and end my own life, or I could set us both free and leave town together. Or, I could wait for Paul, who was due soon, and have it out with him.

"I sat in my chair next to the small cage for two days and then just before daylight today made my decision. I would end this nightmare. Andre was still asleep propped up in his bed. I quietly opened the cage retrieved the gun and aimed it. Just as I pulled the trigger, Chance stepped in front of the cage and the gun went off." At this point, Gladys looked straight at the man she had always considered her son and continued.

"There is no apology great enough to ask for your forgiveness but I owe you gratitude for forcing me to never forgive myself." She then turned and finished her story.

"I think all of you now know enough details to charge both Andre and I. I will say no more without a lawyer. Would it be possible for me to speak to my husband today, Captain?"

The chief was blown away. How could all of this happen in little old Branfield? Why would his son, Adam want to get involved and where in the world was he now? He'd probably be called to testify. Why didn't he, himself, listen more carefully to Octavia and her cohorts?

Finally, who would or should be charged with what? Well, that's why they have paid me the big bucks all of these years and he called Lt. Davis.

"Yes sir. This is Lieutenant Carl Davis. What do you need, Chief?" He answered when the call came into his patrol car. "I'm over at the mansion right now; just trying to get more information about affairs of last week."

"That's a good idea, Carl. I am going to have to take this whole crew down to the station. That means Andre Gertz, Gladys Gertz, Morris Chance, Luther Banks and Jessica Gilmore. Captain Cahill from the State Police will come with me. We're going to split up the people involved and use three cars so as not to be noticed too much in town. At this point I believe that all five will be charged with something but we're going to have to do a lot more talking and I'm sure all will be accompanied by a personal lawyer before long. We're in for it, Carl.

"I want you to be our third car. You will be carrying Gladys and Jessica. Do not talk to them about this. You will be going right back to this site as soon as possible. I want to leave you in charge of the crime site." Jim said. "Are there other State Police on site? And, are our two detectives, Herm and Donny, being very careful to record every move they make? I can't stress enough that I believe this thing will blow up way past anything Branfield has ever witnessed so make sure to take copious notes and endless photos. Do not interview anyone out there. If anybody does need to be queried bring them down to the station. Is that clear?'

"Yes sir. Yes, I gave Herm and Donny your orders and will inform them about what is going on now. If Capt. Cahill thinks it's OK, I'd recommend that we get at least 4 more men to help here."

"I'll do that right away. Once you deliver your prisoners, let me know when you think your people have done all they can, then make sure the place is securely locked and guarded before bringing your info to the station. Again I say, don't talk to anyone not already involved.

Thanks Carl. I expect we'll be at this for days so make plans." The chief hung up and headed for the living room.

"OK everyone, could I have your attention please. We've decided that there's enough goings on here that we'll have to take all of you to the station. That means you may want to call your lawyers right now or wait until you see if any charges are made. I will be taking Morris Chance and Luther Banks, with me, Capt. Cahill will escort Andre, and Lt. Davis will bring Ms. Gilmore and Mrs. Gertz with him. We are hoping our cars will not be noticed but..."

The accused used the next hour to make calls to family or friends and then all except Gladys contacted their lawyers in hopes that they would meet them at Branfield's Police Station.

Within a week, Andre and Gladys were charged with kidnapping, child abuse and endangerment; Gladys was also charged with intent to murder. Morris George Chance was charged with kidnapping and imprisonment. Both Jessica Gilmore and Luther Banks were not charged but were required to stay within recall distance should there be a trial.

The town of Branfield instantly became the talk of the world. As predicted by Luther, the whole thing was to rival Barnum and Bailey. Within two days the streets were filled with TV trucks and gawkers. By the end of the week the entertainment channels had arrived and the Chief had to limit the number of STRAGGLER fans to 400 per day. By the third week after the charges were made, he also issued curfews for all main streets in the town.

Separate trial dates were set for Andre, Gladys, and Morris while Luther and Jessie were fined and released on their own recognizance and required to be ready to testify when needed. Due to the seriousness of the crimes Andre and Gladys Gertz were not granted bail but a bail amount of $500,000 was set and met immediately by Morris.

For many years, the town had been able to deal with crimes in the small court room in their town hall. It was obvious that that would not suffice and after much legal wrangling the trials of Andre, Gladys and Morris, were scheduled to be held in the Hillsboro County court house about 20 mile away. The highways from the town to the courthouse were jammed for the whole month of August.

CHAPTER XVII
EPILOGUE

"Well, OK. Here we are at BETTY'S, the trial has come to a halt, and September is almost out of the picture. What are we going to do now?' Marion began. "I'm just blown away."

"Can you believe it? Our little town, soon to be city, splashed all over the world? What a trial this has been. I'm so glad all of us could see it." Octavia exclaimed.

"I guess I am too but still can't believe the details. How in the world could we have missed the whole thing so easily? Was it just because we were so busy with practically nothing?" Marion chimed in."

"I know what you mean, Mare." Martha put in. "Here we were thinking our problems were tough when a really big crime was right

183

under our noses. Not only that but we were beginning to fancy ourselves as real detectives. Hah! By the way, what surprised you the most about the events in the trial, Marth?"

"Well, I guess the fact that Adam had been sort of involved. I was totally hit sideways when his two friends were called to tell what they knew and Adam was fined such a large amount. I'd guess the Army may get involved. That has got to be a blow for Jim, Octavia. Will he be OK? This Chance was very thorough you have to admit; getting the chief's son to turn off the security was a heck of an idea."

"As you can imagine, it certainly was a surprise for Jimmy." Olivia interrupted. He often says 'The minute you think you have already seen everything, it's time to stop being a cop.' This saying sure backed that up. It might be enough to shake some sense into that Adam, I hope. I guess the most surprising thing for me, even though we've all read books about women and love, I would never have believed that good old straight laced Gladys would have fallen so far. Do we lose our ability to tell right from wrong if the right man comes along?"

"I kind of wish all of this had never happened." Marion put in. "I really did think that this town was different from the rest of the world. What pie in the sky! It's quite a come down to realize that we're so mundane. Imagine! We've just heard of a near murder, a politician hell-bent on winning regardless of the cause, racial bias, and child abuse at its worst. Not in my town, I would have said a few months ago."

"And, you forgot to mention that one of the world's biggest stars grew up in our small berg; a lot of eye-openers in the last two years. I know it wouldn't be fair to say I was glad to have it come along, but it was great not to be constantly reminded of COVID." Martha said. "So, what do you two think will be the verdict? They say the judge will hear arguments and recommendations from the jury. Then rule on September 24th. If guilty, which seems to me to be the only way to go, what should the punishment be? And, what do we think will become of Chance's Stragglers? My kids love that band."

"Well, I'd say Chance has an open and shut case for putting Andre and Gladys in jail for life. I know he has declined to testify against Gladys as far as the shooting goes, but I'm sure she might get some extra years for attempted manslaughter or for trying to shoot good ol' Andre. As far as he goes I'd say guilty and throw away the key; no chance of parole." Marion threw in. "And Hal agrees. We both feel it's time for all of our citizens to pay more attention to the politicians in Branfield and the state."

"I have to say that Chance is a handsome son of a gun. Lithe, six feet plus and that blond hair! It's enough to make a woman swoon." Octavia said enthusiastically.

"There you go again, Tave. I guess the fact that Paul/Morris/Chance made those drawings and kept all of the other records will put them away for a long time. As for Chance, I'm betting on a very light penalty of some kind; maybe with parole. I hope so." said Martha. "As for town politics, I'm thinking that maybe we should join one of the major parties in town and carry signs or march, or whatever they need while we're all spry enough." She added.

"Could be, but I have had another idea for us. To be honest I don't really enjoy all the clandestine stuff. I don't even think we're very good at the detective business and so I was ruminating about us last night and have come up with an idea. I know it will come way out of left field, but please hear me out." Octavia said enthusiastically.

Both of her friends bought another glass of iced tea and though rolling their eyes, settled down to listen.

"What we need is a new and different goal in our lives. We're getting on and I believe I've come up with just the thing. We are all intelligent, thoughtful women who seem to have similar views about the idiosyncrasies of the human race Why not share our ideas?" Octavia went on.

'I don't know about that." said Marion. "All I've done in life is keeping records, plan lessons for the kids, or write up copy for Hal and the museum. Well, I did raise a couple of wondrous kids."

185

Without a pause Octavia went on. "In addition, we have time on our hands and plenty of juicy information from this trial. I think it's time for three lifetime citizens to write a book about the whole thing from a citizen's point of view. And, more than that, from a woman's point of view. Imagine the headline: SMALL TOWN WOMEN AND BIG TIME CRIME or THE POLITICAL CHILD ABUSER, or HOW LONG SHOULD A WIFE STICK WITH HER MAN? Or..."

"Stop, Tavia. Pull yourself together. Us? Write a book? Would we publish it? What would our better halves say? I admit I do know a lot about organizing from setting up the restaurant, but still...I sure have been surprised at the things that have gone on in my little town.

"Wait. Are those brownies over there? I feel the need for a couple." Marion said as she rushed off to the counter.

"I have to admit, Octave, You've certainly thrown us a curve ball this time but maybe it has some possibilities. Dennis would be happy to see me busy again. We've had a devil of a time dealing with the fact that I got so involved in the town's doings without his knowledge.

"He wants to go back to work at the hospital for a couple more years. I've been wondering what I could do and really didn't want to get involved in the kid's affairs or for that matter anymore crime stuff. Write a book? Three of us? Could that be done without killing each other? How would we begin? I don't know if we'd want to put in the time."

"Oh my gosh Martha. Those look so good! Just what we need-a sweet to calm us down." Martha said as she took two brownies from the plate her friend set on the table.

"I tell you what ladies; let's do what we always do: go home and think long and hard about this and then meet next Wednesday to see if we want to tackle anything new. I do have a friend in Boston who would give me some advice as to how three people could go about this and I still hope we'll decide to give it a try." Octavia as they said good bye.

"Please don't just dismiss this. See you next week my fellow authors. Oh. And bring a pen or a tablet so that we can get started. Bye."

"Amazing how persuasive that woman can be." Her two friends said in unison.

END

BEVERLY A. MASSEY

ACKNOWLEDGEMENTS

Who could write a novel without the encouragement of those around them? Not I. After reviewing my first encounters with the written word, I even wonder if Shakespeare wouldn't quale at the idea. Certainly, it takes a lot of self-confidence to attack such a task and a great deal of mine comes from those around me.

A giant thank you to my husband, Bob who almost never complained about the endless hours I spent fretting over words and ideas. I also offer my thanks to my sister, Betty Tyson and my family for holding me up when I was sure the fireplace would be a good place for my efforts.

I must thank the reviewers at Readers' Favorite as well. I appreciated their gentle criticisms as well as their helpful suggestions.

Finally, big thanks to my son, Tim, for all of the time he spent rescuing me from my computer's idiosyncrasies as I toiled on a manuscript.

ABOUT THE AUTHOR

Beverly A. Massey was born in Manchester, New Hampshire, in 1932. Her family soon moved to Goffstown, NH where she attended Goffstown High and then graduated from UNH. In 1954 she married Robert A. Massey. They raised four children and then moved to Florida where they have lived for 40 years.

In Florida, Ms. Massey earned a Master's Degree and taught English at Daytona Beach Community College and at New Smyrna Beach High for many years.

HEARTLESS AMBITION is her second novel. She has also written a memoir entitled, LIFE IN BEV'S LANE, a book of essays with Betty Tyson and Nancy Greenleaf, entitled, A CAUCUS OF OLD CROWS, and a fictional novel entitled, TARNISHED.

CPSIA information can be obtained
at www.ICGtesting.com
Printed in the USA
BVHW082203130922
646893BV00010B/716

Heartless Ambition by Beverly A. Massey is a slice-of-life story that demonstrates how even seemingly innocuous towns can have hidden secrets... It accurately portrays a small town in America, with gossiping women, talkative bar owners, rebellious youngsters, and selfish politicians manipulating their way to the top. The characters are colorful, with distinct personalities and motives that leave a mark on the reader. The author takes her time to set up the characters and let the plot get into the groove. I especially enjoyed the dialogue, as it genuinely felt like how people talk in small towns across America. Highly recommended.
★★★★★　　　　　　FIVE STAR REVIEW Pikasho Deka for Readers' Favorite

It takes one bigot to cause societal havoc. This is the premise behind **Heartless Ambition** by Beverly A. Massey. The town of Branfield, New Hampshire takes pride in the fact that their humble town is special. But the townspeople will wake up one day to realize that their town ...is not immune to societal evils as Andre Jan Gertz assumes the mayoral position and has ambition set on becoming a senator. Reading Heartless Ambition is a thrilling and satisfying experience for its reliable narration and gossipy dialogues among the townsfolk. Beverly A. Massey infuses the storyline with her own brand of storytelling that shows a fondness for characters that makes the storyline larger-than-life as they express their sentiments on how one man changes their town for the worse... Heartless Ambition is a must-read because it doesn't stop at character studies. It is also a reflection of the great lengths that one is willing to go in the name of self-interest.
★★★★★　　　　　　FIVE STAR REVIEW Vincent Dublado for Readers' Favorite

As a treatise on power and the ability of power to corrupt, the author created a wonderful character in Andre Paul Gertz...The plot contains enough red herrings and twists and turns to keep the reader invested...until the end.
★★★★　　　　　　FOUR STAR REVIEW　Grant Leishman for Readers' Favorite

Though fictional, stories like this reflect reality and reveal how dark the human soul can become if left unrestrained and allowed to give in completely to narcissistic desires.
★★★★　　　　　　FOUR STAR REVIEW　by Foluso Falaye for Readers' Favorite

ISBN 979-8-218-05161-7

9 798218 051617　　$13.9

MASTER THE ART OF PLANNING LIVE EVENTS

A Small Business Owners Guide to
Build Your Brand,
Drive Revenue, and
Grow a Sustainable Business

Anza Goodbar